JAM JAM JAM

with
GARY MOORE

Professional Guitar Workshops

CONTENTS

ON THE CD

The CD is split into two sections; section 1 (tracks 1–8) is the backing tracks to the titles listed above. Section 2 (tracks 9–16) is each of the backing tracks listed above with all the lead guitar parts included for your reference, played by Stuart Bull and Richard Barrett.

Music arranged & produced by Stuart Bull and Steve Finch.
Recorded at the TOTAL ACCURACY SOUNDHOUSE, Romford, England.

Stuart Bull: guitar & drums, Richard Barrett: guitar, Gerry Cunningham: bass, Pete Adams: keyboards.

Professional Guitar Workshops

© International Music Publications Ltd
First published in 1996 by International Music Publications Ltd
International Music Publications Ltd is a Faber Music company
Bloomsbury House 74–77 Great Russell Street London WC1B 3DA
Printed in England by Caligraving Ltd
All rights reserved

ISBN10: 0-571-52718-3
EAN13: 978-0-571-52718-2

To buy Faber Music publications or to find out about the full range of titles available, please contact your local music retailer or Faber Music sales enquiries:

Faber Music Ltd, Burnt Mill, Elizabeth Way, Harlow, CM20 2HX England
Tel: +44(0)1279 82 89 82   Fax: +44(0)1279 82 89 83
sales@fabermusic.com   fabermusic.com

Introduction

The TOTAL ACCURACY 'JAM WITH...' series, is a powerful learning tool that will help you extend your stockpile of licks and fills and develop your improvisational skills. The combination of musical notation and guitar tablature in the book together with backing tracks on the CD gives you the opportunity to learn each track note for note and then jam with a professional session band. The track listing reflects some of Gary Moore's most popular recordings, providing something for guitarists to have fun and improvise with, as well as something to aspire to.

The first eight tracks on the CD are full length backing tracks recorded minus lead guitar. The remaining tracks feature the backing tracks with the lead guitar parts added. Although many of you will have all the original tracks in your own collection, we have provided them in the package for your reference. The 'JAM WITH...' series allows you to accurately recreate the original, or to use the transcriptions in this book in conjunction with the backing tracks as a basis for your own improvisation. For your benefit we have put definite endings on most of the backing tracks, rather than fading these out as is the case on some of the original recordings. The accompanying transcriptions correspond to our versions. Remember, experimenting with your own ideas is equally important for developing your own style; most important of all however is that you enjoy JAM with GARY MOORE and HAVE FUN!

Gary Moore made his first stage appearance at the age of three singing at his father's club in Dublin. He first started playing the guitar when he was ten, after his father bought a guitar from one of the club's musicians. In the first week he had learned *Wonderful Land* by The Shadows and his playing took on even more significance the moment he heard John Mayall's definitive 'Blues-breakers' album with Eric Clapton on guitar.

Influenced by Jeff Beck with the Yardbirds, Jimi Hendrix, and the melodic compositions of The Beatles, Moore joined his first band, Dave and the Diamonds. Soon after, he moved on to form his own blues band, Platform Three, and then, while still in his teens, he became a member of Skid Row, his first professional band. The 'freaky singer' of the band was of course Phil Lynott and the two went on to enjoy a string of successes. In 1978 Moore's first solo album *Back On The Streets* was recorded. It was a fusion of hard rock, blues, heavy metal and pop and featured his infamous *Parisienne Walkways*. In 1979 Moore once again worked with Phil Lynott on the Thin Lizzy 'Black Rose' Tour.

In Dublin, Moore had the chance to meet his all time idol, Fleetwood Mac's Peter Green. Moore considered Green "… the greatest blues player to come out of everywhere". The album *Still Got The Blues* is a testament to the wasted talent of Peter Green and is dedicated to him. One of Moore's guitars, probably used extensively on this album, is a Gold Top Les Paul, given to him by Peter Green.

On the album, Moore experienced the chance to forget writing, recording, rehearsing, touring - the year in, year out circus of professional music - and simply enjoyed playing the guitar again. That is the reason why a lot of the album is done totally live. He had the pleasure to play with Albert Collins on *Too Tired* and 57 year old Albert King on a cover of King's classic record *Oh Pretty Woman*. Albert King has reputedly said of Moore "Gary plays like his fingers are on fire. He plays rock and blues and I call his style a kind of rock blues thing". The combination of covers and original material on *Still Got The Blues* coincided perfectly with the British blues revival of that year.

Gary Moore's musical projects have consisted of jazz rock, heavy rock and several soulful ballads. However many recent tracks, including *Story Of The Blues* from the album *After Hours,* have taken him back to his blues roots.

Performance Notes

Still Got The Blues

Utilising a strong 'hook' melody on the solo guitar, then developing to a more improvised approach without ever forgetting the main theme, this ballad is played mainly on the neck pickup of a Gibson Les Paul. Like the majority of Gary's most recent work in the blues style, there are no multiple layers of guitar, but one single track which sounds as though it was recorded in one 'pass', using the guitar's volume control to achieve changes in dynamics from full-on-scream to short rhythmic stabs. In fact the only evidence of overdubbing is the quiet arpeggiated guitar, similar in style to Parisienne Walkways.

Most of the solo work, both in the main theme and the later improvised passages, uses the A minor pentatonic scale (A,C,D,E,G) and the A natural minor scale (A,B,C,D,E,F,G,A). Gary also makes a brief foray into the A harmonic minor scale (A,B,C,D,E,F,G#,A) during the outro solo. At this point Gary shifts to the bridge pickup for a while, once again changing the dynamics of the track before returning to the neck pickup for the return of the main theme.

Walking By Myself

This up-tempo R&B track is one of the few recordings to feature a driving distorted rhythm guitar part which uses chromatic blues runs between some chord changes, for example between the E and B chords at the end of the verse sections the melody is E,G#,A,Bb,B. There is some quite an aggressive soloing using the E blues scale (E,G,A,Bb,B,D) and string bends combined with double stops to create an even raunchier sound. This effect is also heightened by a medium room echo and a short 'slapback' delay providing the illusion (at the time probably no illusion at all!) of great volume.

Wide string bends and lightning fast blues licks are featured prominently - also some other tricks which hark back to Gary's 'rock' days - trilling between open and fretted notes (in this case on the B string), muting blues scale runs and pinch harmonics are all featured here.

The track ends with a squealing string bend on the 22nd fret of the top E string, some characteristic string handling noise, and a massive E7#9 chord.

The Loner

This track has a very 'produced' sound to it, but Gary's guitar - in this case probably a Charvel with a Floyd Rose tremelo and EMG pickups - retains a raw distorted tone. Throughout the track the phrasing is executed in a careful and restrained manner and for the most part the tremelo is only used to add a subtle vibrato. After the initial statement of the melody line it is repeated an octave higher for the following section. Things begin to change when some consecutive string bends are played high up the fretboard. These will require careful attention to sound right and not out of tune. Timing is also of the essence during this section. The melody then re-emerges in part, raised by still another octave, bringing this section to a climax.

At this point the guitar changes role, playing some decorative - though still melodic - fills. As this section progresses the fills become more regular and freestyle, developing on the idea of fast pentatonic themes repeating with a new twist each time. It is only towards the end of the track that the faster playing enters the picture. The melody or main theme is based around the G natural minor scale (G,A,Bb,C,D,Eb,F,G) and the improvisations nearer the end use all five positions of the G minor pentatonic scale (G,Bb,C,D,F).

Oh Pretty Woman

Using the classic combination of a Vintage Les Paul and Marshall amplifiers, reputedly aided by a Marshall Guvnor distortion pedal, the searing lead tone on this track is one of Gary's most emulated sounds. By contrast Albert King's sharp tone, from a custom built Gibson 'flying V', is hardly distorted at all, but sounds just as urgent thanks to the wide string bends and vibrato which punctuate his economical phrasing.

Both guitarists rely heavily on the C minor pentatonic scale (C,Eb,F,G,Bb) in various positions across the fretboard. This song provides an excellent showcase for Gary Moore's playing, mixing soulful blues bends with frantic rock pentatonic ideas.

Some of the faster picked sections are executed by dragging the pick across adjacent strings while using the blues scale, rather than strict alternate picking. Hammer-on's and Pull-off's are also strongly in evidence, especially on the end of the track.

Story Of The Blues

Like most of these blues recordings a Gibson Les Paul and Marshall Amp were used, although here Gary is using a slightly sharper tone than he uses on other tracks. Throughout this song the solo guitar punctuates the vocal with classic double stop blues phrases - mournful string bends and percussive chord stabs, occasionally letting up for the chorus with some power chords - while also doubling the clean arpeggiated guitar for a short time.

The solo on this track reaches epic proportions mainly using the A blues scale (A,C,D,D#,E,G). There are some blindingly fast passages, not so much alternate picked, but played with a sweeping motion across the strings, to provide seemingly effortless speed and articulation. Some of the string bends require quite a lot of hand strength, particuarily where Gary bends from a C at the 20th fret of the top E string way up to an E!

To end the track the guitar's volume control is 'backed-off' slightly to achieve a cleaner sound, and the whole song shifts down a gear for a quiet ending, although on the original recording this is still loud enough to generate feedback on the final note.

Cold Day In Hell

On this track the guitar alternates between blues fills and chunky chord backing, using a moderately distorted, sharp tone. Like many of the bluesier tracks, the guitar seems to have been played as a whole live 'take' rather than having been overdubbed in stages. The soloing from this song is more from the 'blues' stable than on some of the others, using the C# blues scale (C#,E,F#,G#,B), while avoiding his trademark blistering runs.

There is wide vibrato and a hard attack featured on all the solo work here, alongside some punchy, muted blues scale passages at the low end and staccato phrasing with pinch harmonics. This track leaves you with the impression that the spaces between the phrases are as important as the phrases themselves.

Empty Rooms

Probably played on a Fender Stratocaster the guitar's role is quite minimal to begin with on this track, only appearing at the end of the first verse playing some soulful string bends and tasteful double stop fills quite far back in the mix. Up to the middle section the song stays in the key of D minor, but changes to a clean almost classical sounding solo section (this has actually been re-recorded since using a classical guitar), the phrasing here is again very minimal, resulting in a strong melody line at times very reminiscent of the kind of phrasing used in Irish folk music and is a definite Gary Moore trademark.

Following a similar section played on fretless bass, the main guitar solo comes in using a combination of D minor pentatonic (D,F,G,A,C) and D natural minor (D,E,F,G,A,Bb,C,D). In keeping with the overall mood of this song this solo never goes to far into 'screaming rock' territory, again retaining a strong sense of melody. The end of the track sees the guitar pounding fills under the final chorus, and playing a melodic line using a technique known as 'violining' to play a short melody which resolves to the chord of D major.

Parisienne Walkways

Apparently played using the Gibson Les Paul once owned by Peter Green (which he used to record classics like 'Albatross'), this track was to become Gary Moore's 'anthem' and the long, infinitely sustained note in the middle a trademark of his live performances of this song.

On the original recording this is surprisingly restrained and shows that the inherent sustain of the guitar and the volume of the amp are what is crucial to holding long notes, rather than the amount of distortion.

The scales used here are the A natural minor (A,B,C,D,E,F,G,A), and the A harmonic minor (A,B,C,D,E,F,G#,A). In fact, harmonically speaking the melody is deceptively complicated, among others using the B diminished scale (B,C,D#,E,F#,G,A,B) over the B major chord which precedes the long sustained note. Many of the string bends in this track have no vibrato applied, though others have a Gary Moore trademark sharp or gradually introduced vibrato.

Notation & Tablature explained

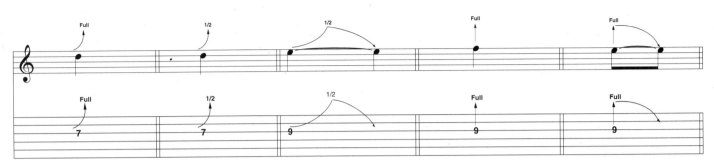

BEND: Strike the note and bend up a whole step (two frets)

BEND: Strike the note and bend up a half step (one fret)

BEND AND RELEASE: Strike the note, bend up a half step, then release the bend.

PRE-BEND: Bend the note up, then strike it

PRE-BEND AND RELEASE: Bend up, strike the note, then release it

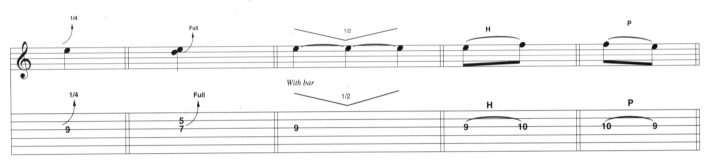

QUARTER-TONE BEND: Bend the note slightly sharp

UNISON BEND: Strike both notes, then bend the lower note up to the pitch of the higher one

TREMOLO BAR BENDS: Strike the note, and push the bar down and up by the amounts indicated

HAMMER-ON: Strike the first note, then sound the second by fretting it without picking

PULL-OFF: Strike the higher note, then pull the finger off while keeping the lower one fretted

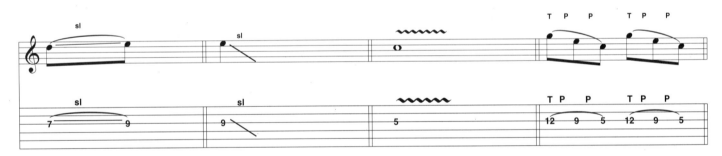

SLIDE: Slide the finger from the first note to the second. Only the first note is struck

SLIDE: Slide to the fret from a few frets below or above

VIBRATO: The string is vibrated by rapidly bending and releasing a note with the fretboard hand or tremolo bar

TAPPING: Hammer on to the note marked with a T using the picking hand, then pull off to the next note, following the hammer-ons or pull-offs in the normal way

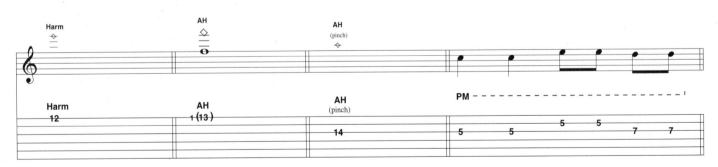

NATURAL HARMONIC: Lightly touch the string directly over the fret shown, then strike the note to create a "chiming" effect

ARTIFICIAL HARMONIC: Fret the note, then use the picking hand finger to touch the string at the position shown in brackets and pluck with another finger

ARTIFICIAL HARMONIC: The harmonic is produced by using the edge of the picking hand thumb to "pinch" the string whilst picking firmly with the plectrum

PALM MUTES: Rest the palm of the picking hand on the strings near the bridge to produce a muted effect. Palm mutes can apply to a single note or a number of notes (shown with a dashed line)

Still Got The Blues

Words and Music by GARY MOORE

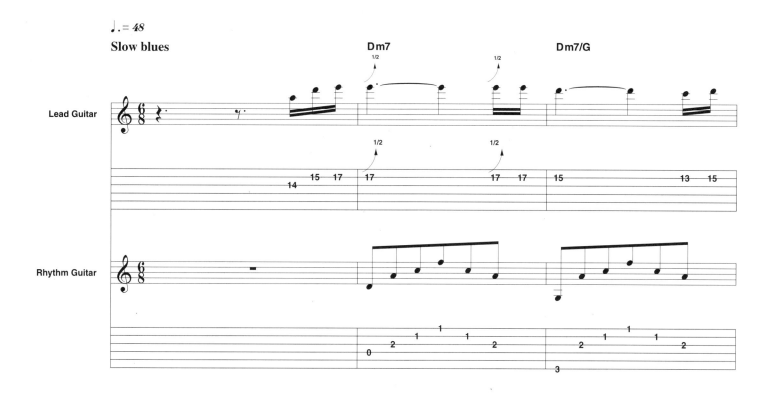

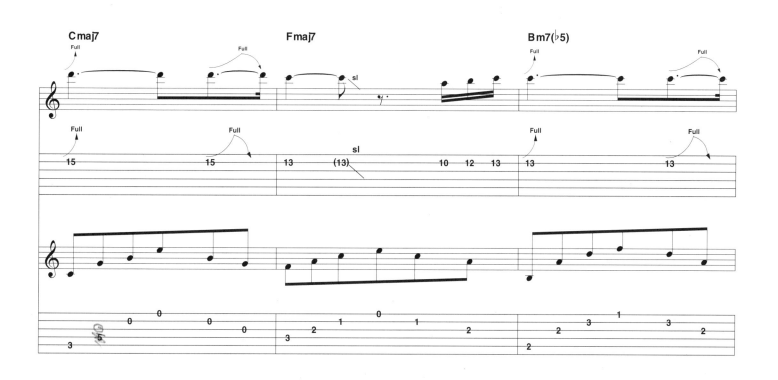

Dm7   Dm7/G   Cmaj7   Fmaj7

1.   Used   to   be   so   ea - sy————,   to   give   my   heart   a - way————,
2.   I   found   out   that   love————,   was   no————   friend   of   mine,

Bm7(♭5)   E7   Am

but   I   found   out   the   hard   way,   there's   a   price————   you   have   to   pay————.
but   I————   should - 've

Bm7(♭5)   E7

known,   time————   af - ter   time————.

Am   Em   Am   D9

So————   long————,   it   was   so————   long—   a - go————,   but   I've

F9   E7   Am

still————   got   the   blues————   for   you————.

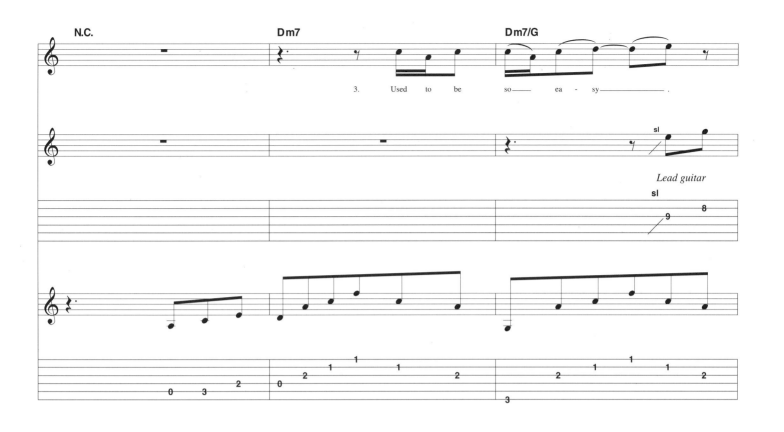

3. Used to be so ea - sy.

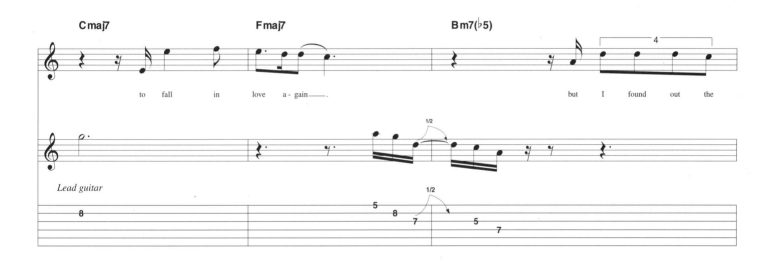

to fall in love a - gain. but I found out the

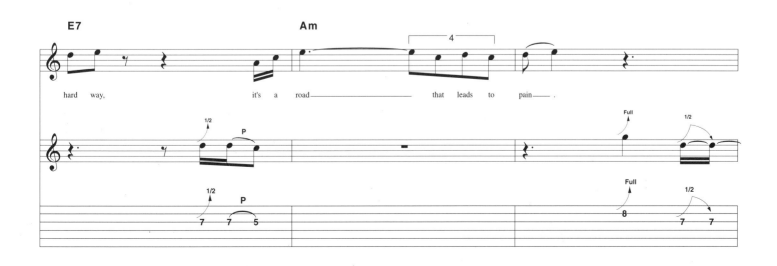

hard way, it's a road that leads to pain.

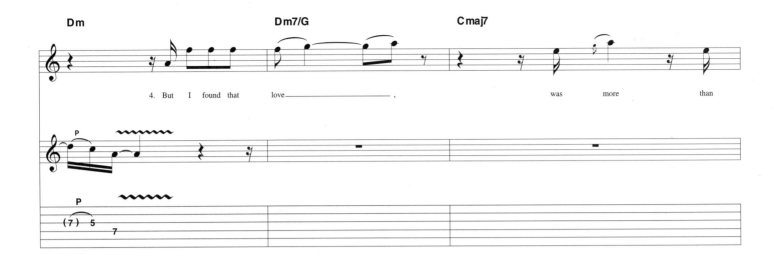

4. But I found that love_____, was more than

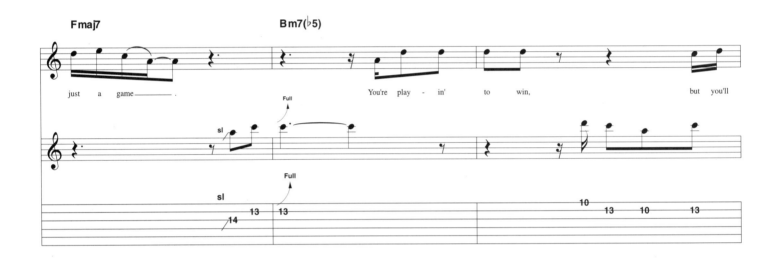

just a game_____. You're play - in' to win, but you'll

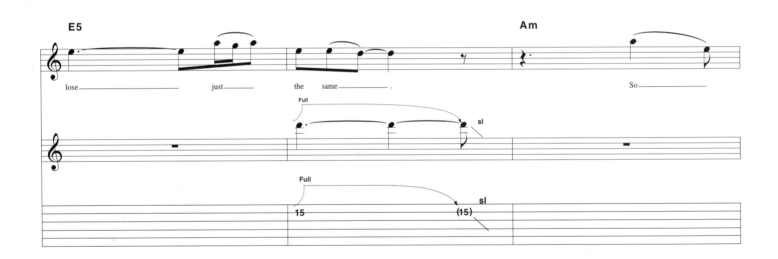

lose_____ just_____ the same_____. So_____

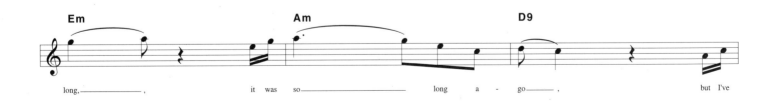

long,_____, it was so_____ long a - go_____, but I've

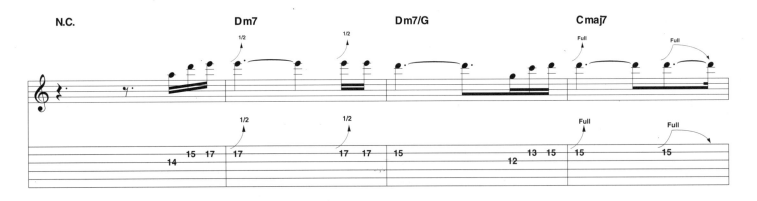

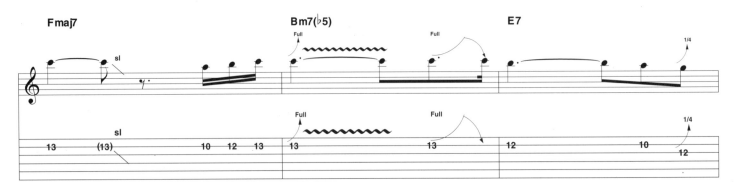

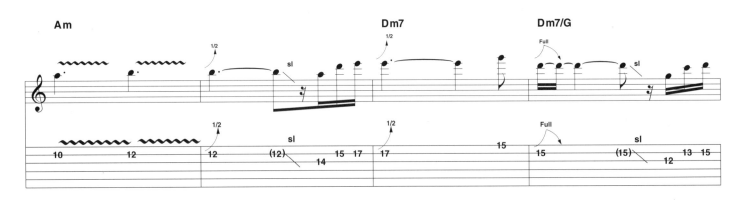

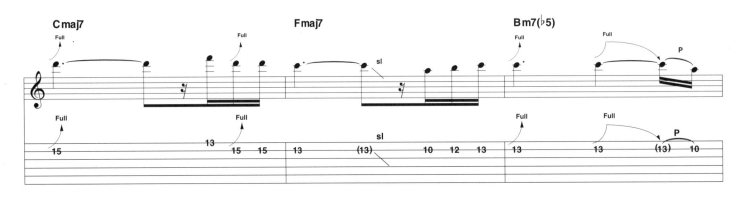

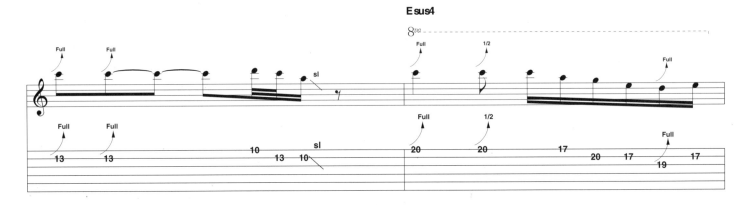

14

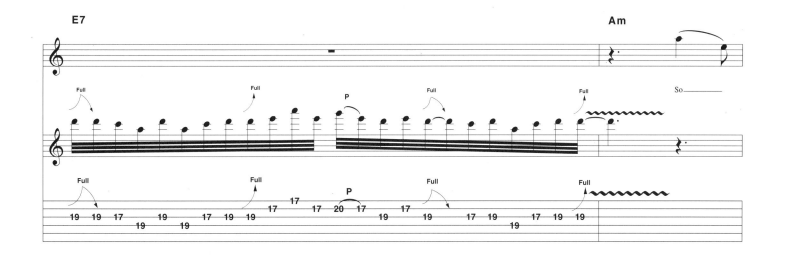

long——, it was so—— long a - go—, but I've still—— got the blues—— for you——.

Though the days—— come and go, there is one—— thing I know——, I've

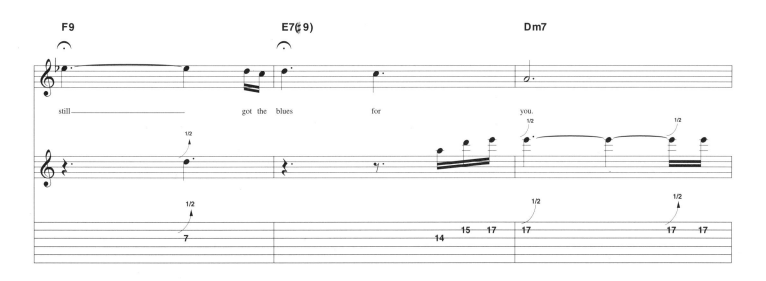

still—————— got the blues for you.

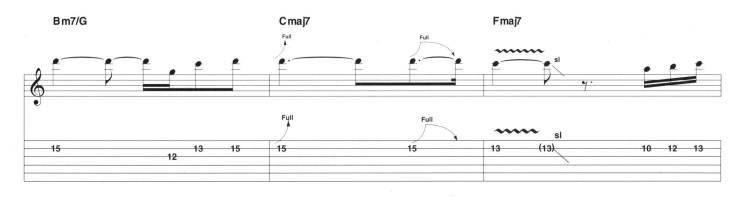

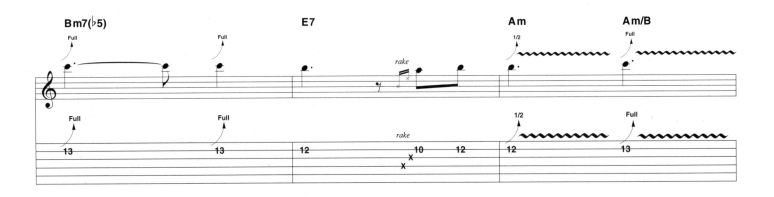

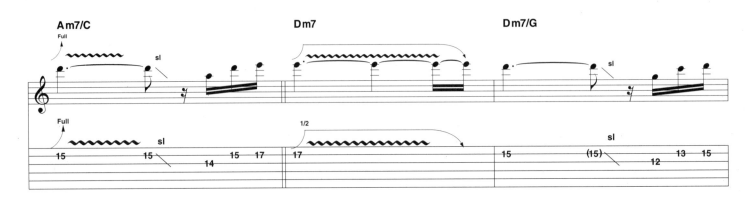

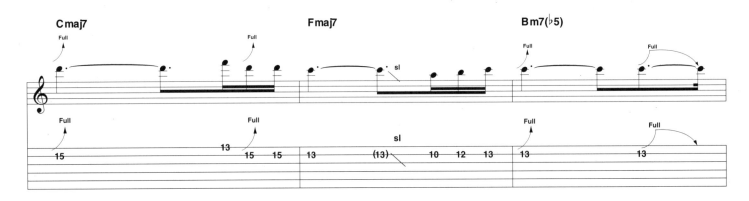

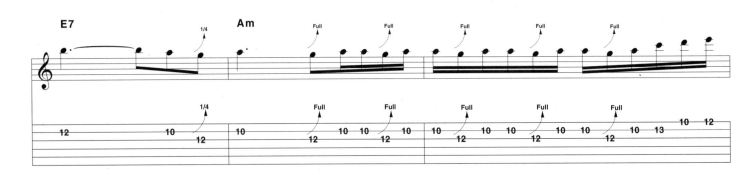

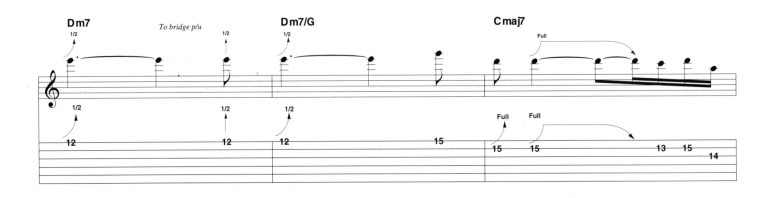

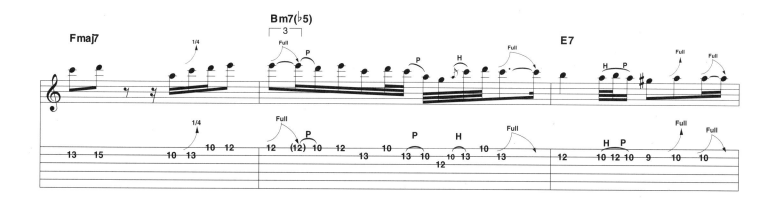

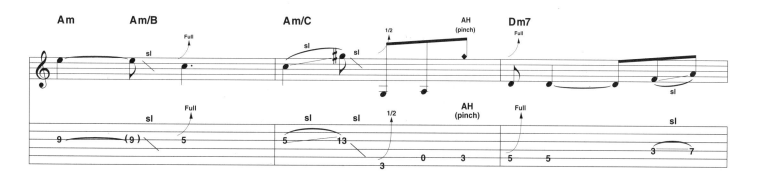

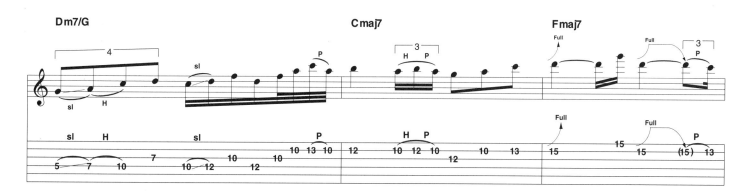

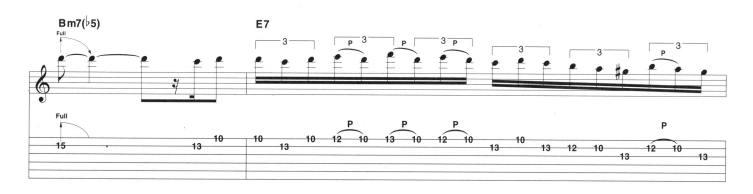

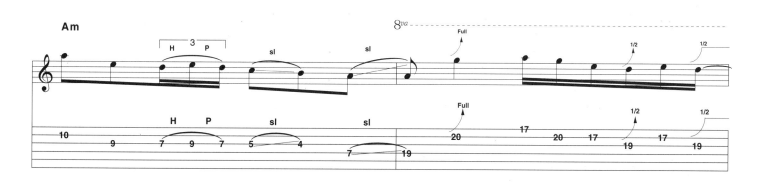

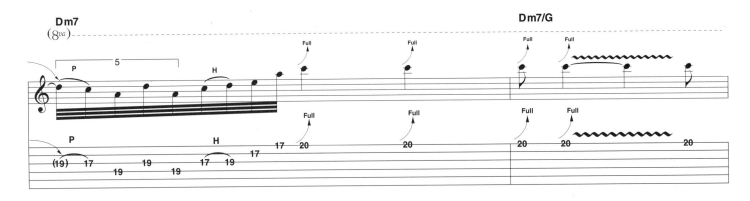

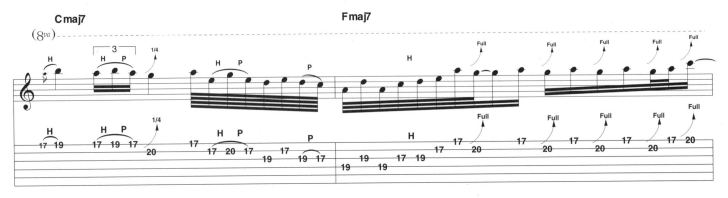

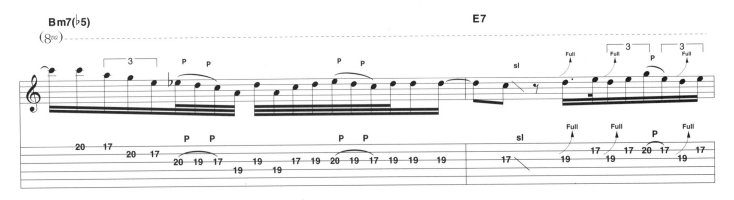

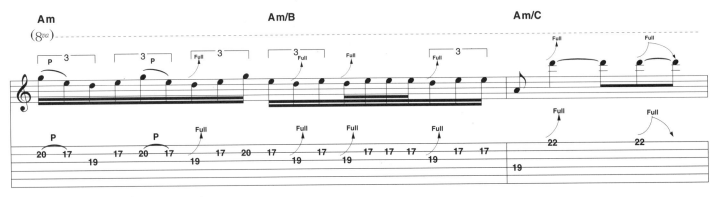

*Rhythm guitar
continues as intro*

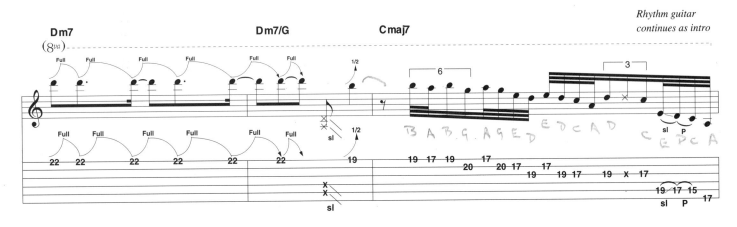

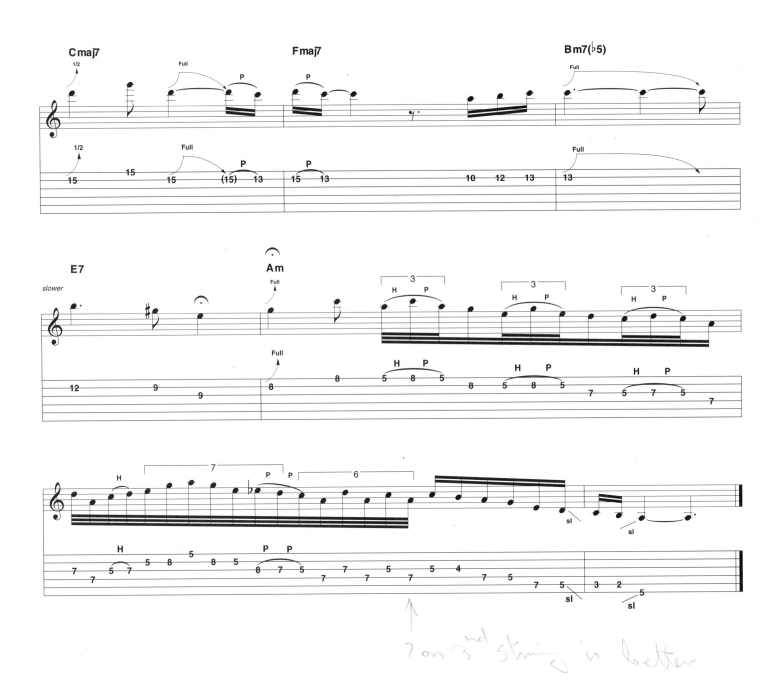

Walking By Myself

Words and Music by JIMMY ROGERS

Give ya all my love babe——, what more——, can I do———?

Walk-in' by my-self I hope you'll un-der-stand——.

I just want to be your lov-er man——.

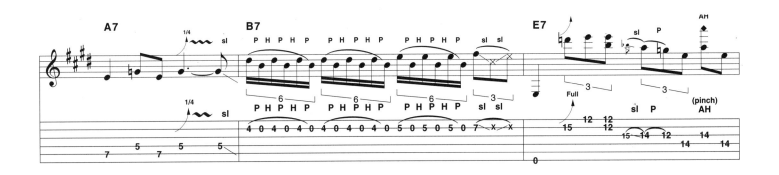

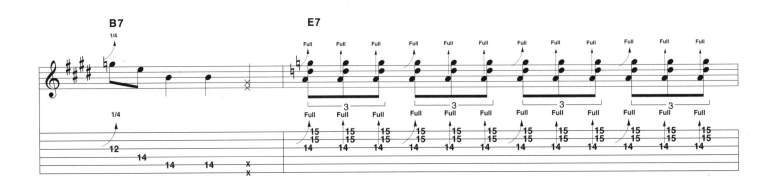

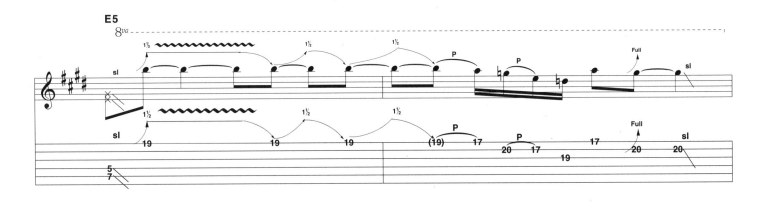

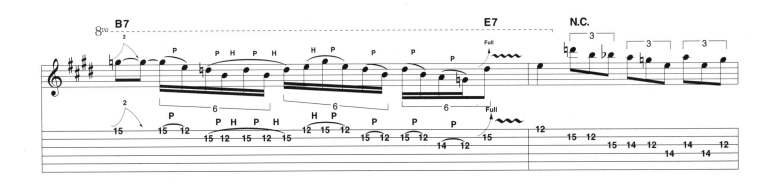

24

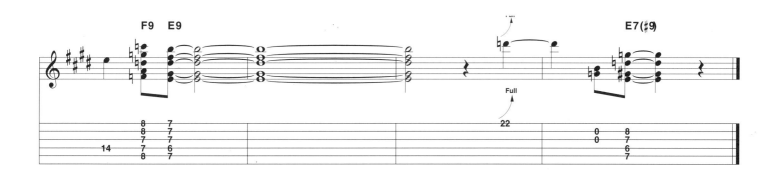

The Loner

Words and Music by MAX MIDDLETON and GARY MOORE

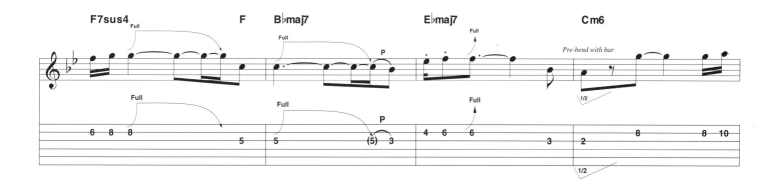

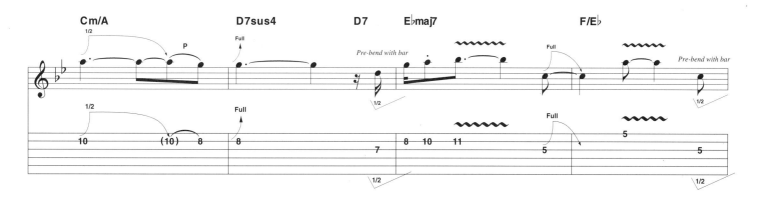

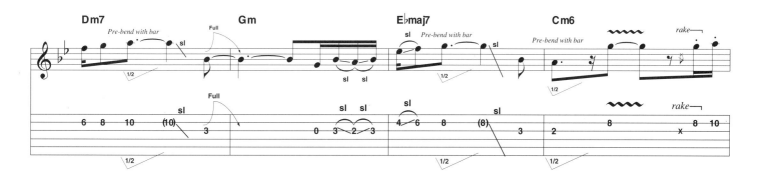

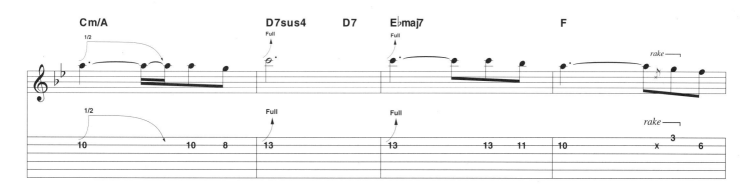

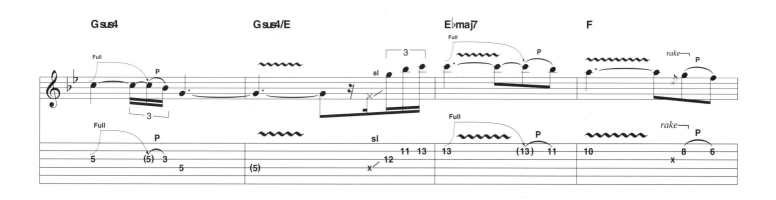

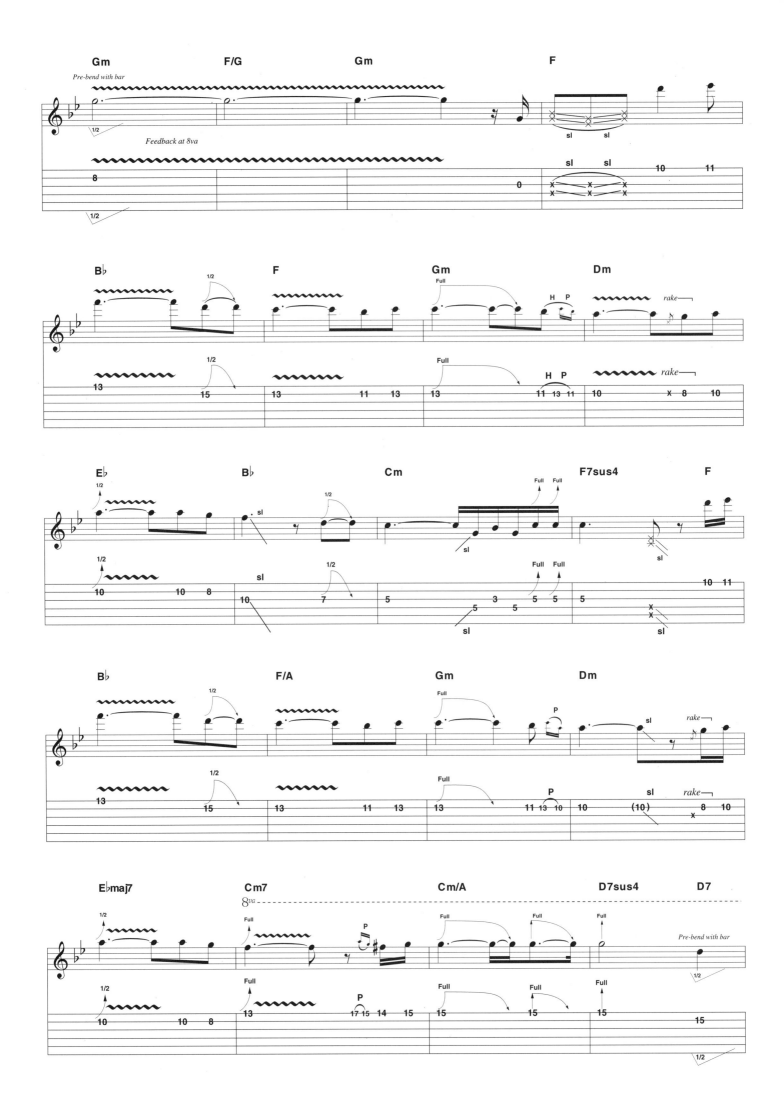

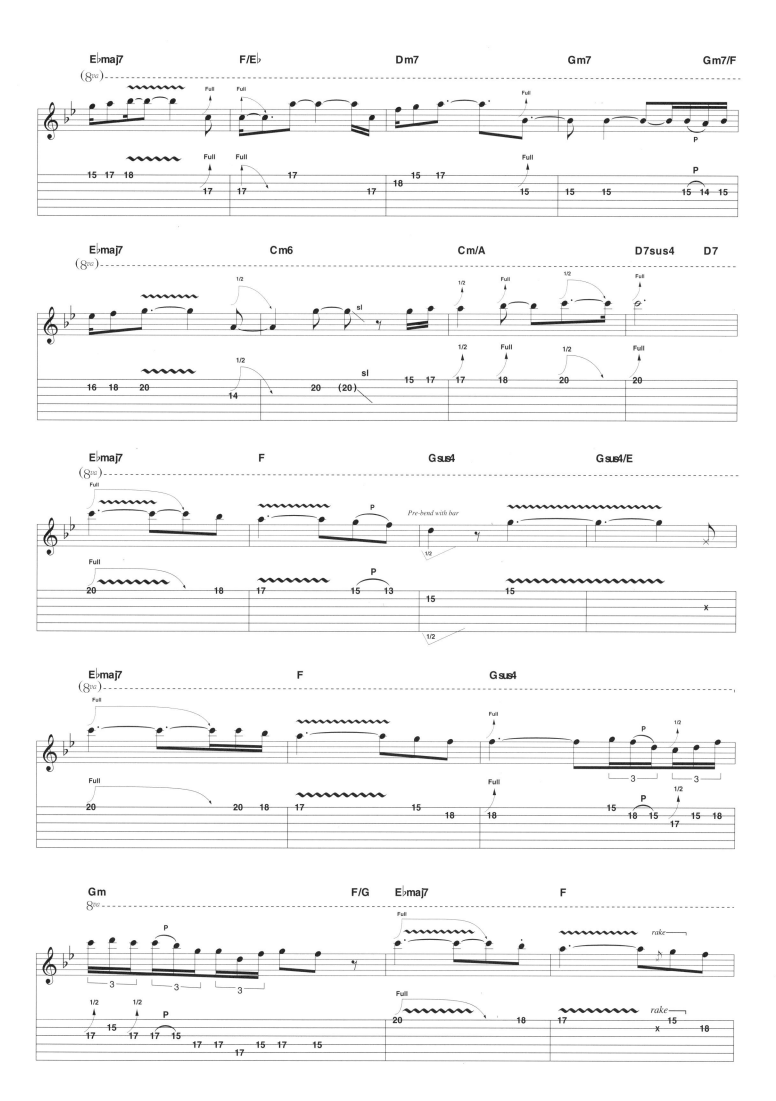

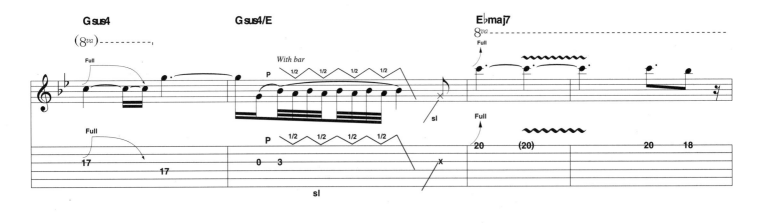

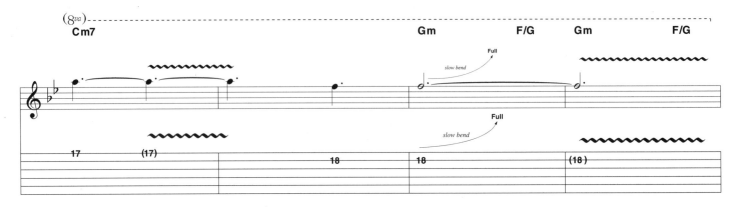

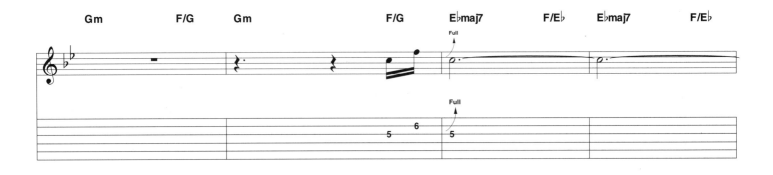

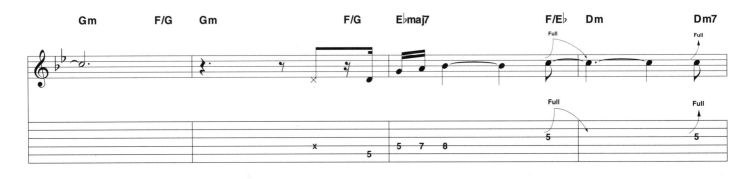

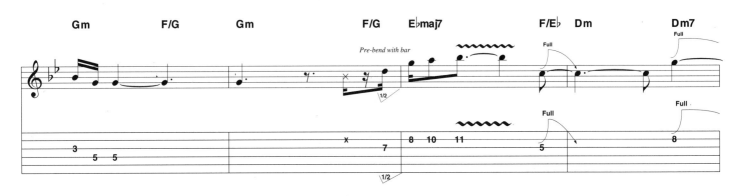

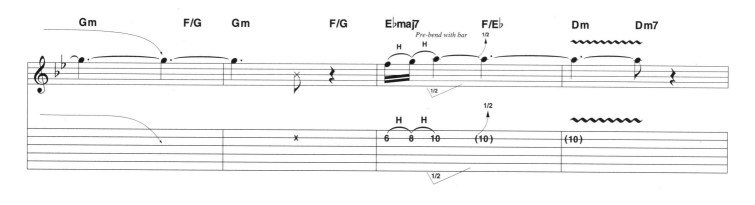

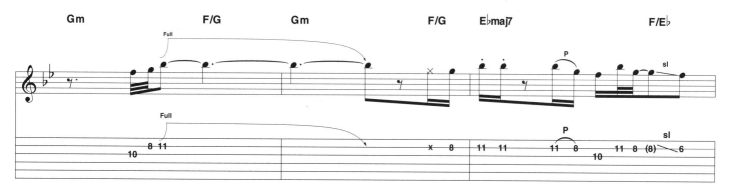

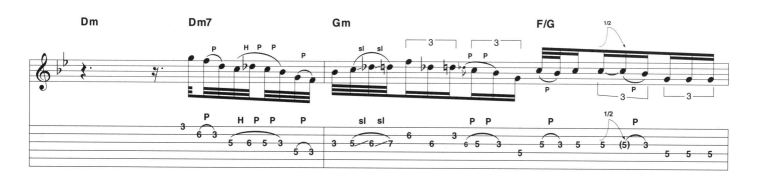

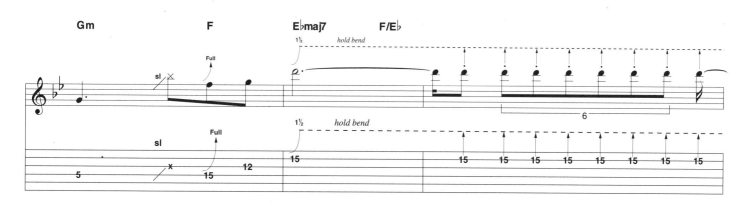

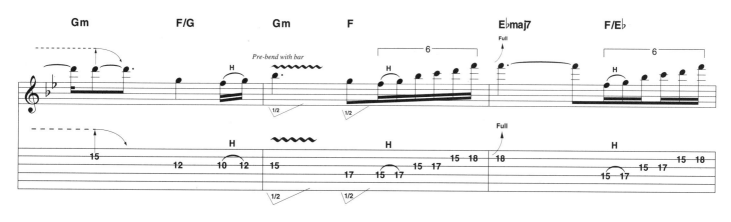

33

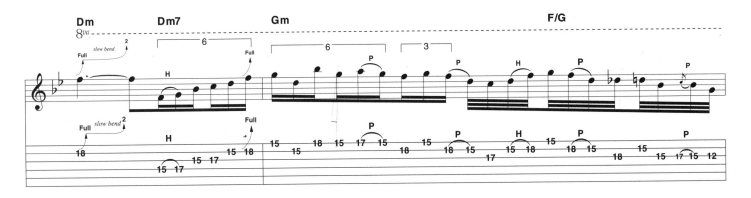

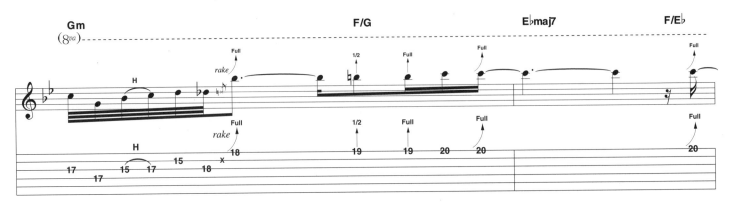

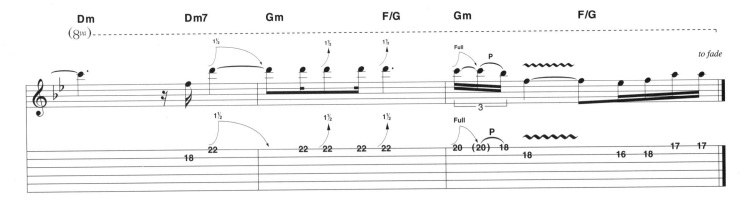

Oh Pretty Woman

Words and Music by A C WILLIAMS

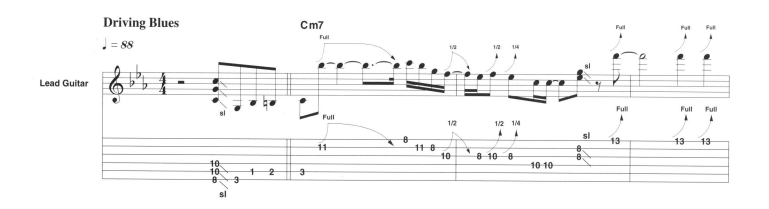

Oh, pret-ty wom-an shows the ris-in' sun—, says all your cheap paint and pow-der ain't goin'

help you none. 'cause she's a pret-ty wom-an right down to her bones— and so you might as well— leave your

(Gary Moore)

(Albert King)

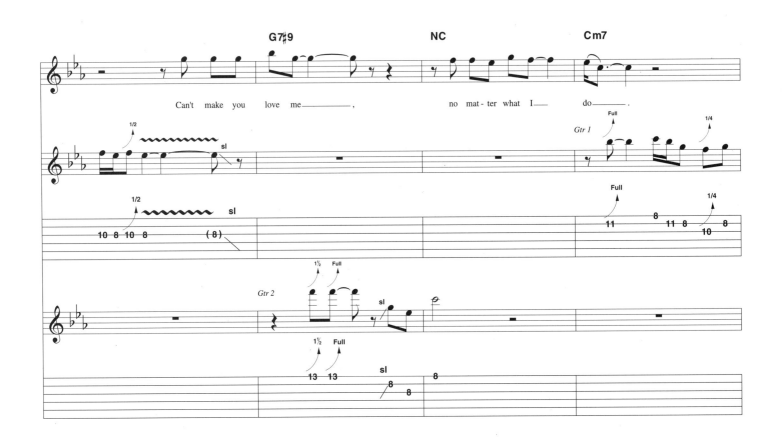

Oh, pret - ty wom - an what - cha gon - na do——? You kept on fool - in' round—— till I got

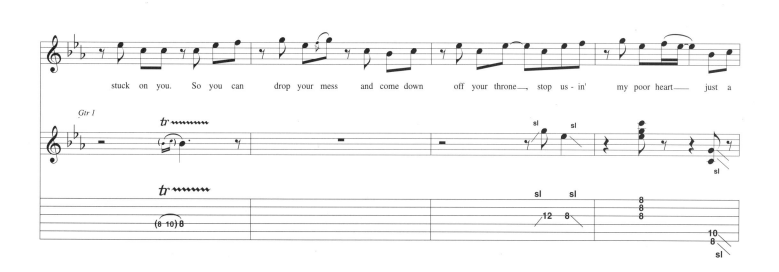

stuck on you. So you can drop your mess and come down off your throne—, stop us - in' my poor heart—— just a

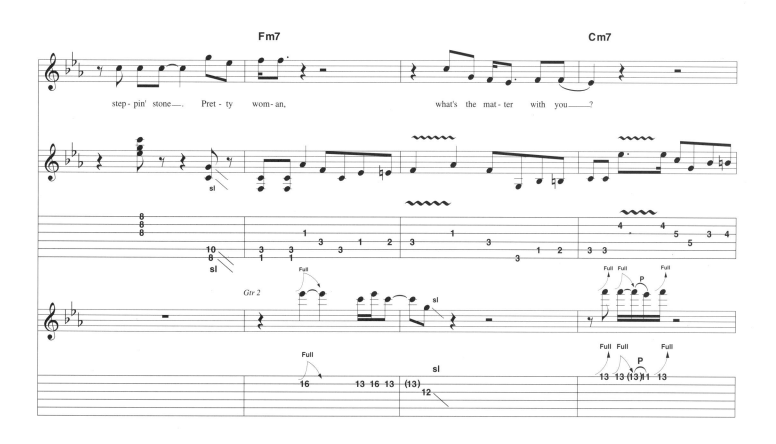

step - pin' stone—. Pret - ty wom - an, what's the mat - ter with you——?

Can't make you love me——, no mat-ter what I—— do——.

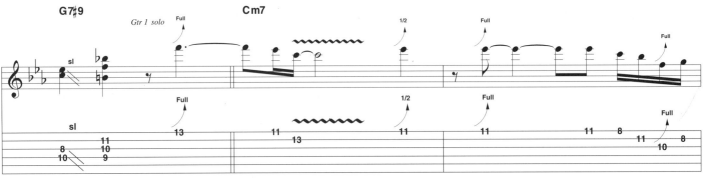

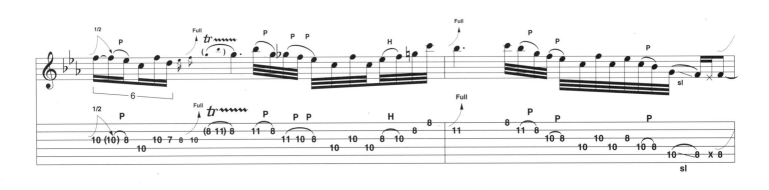

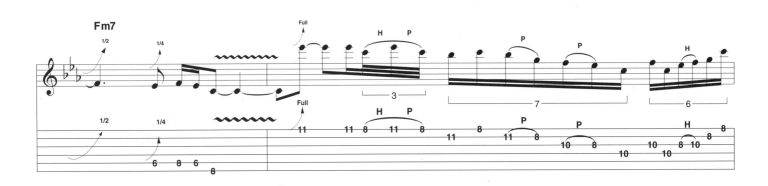

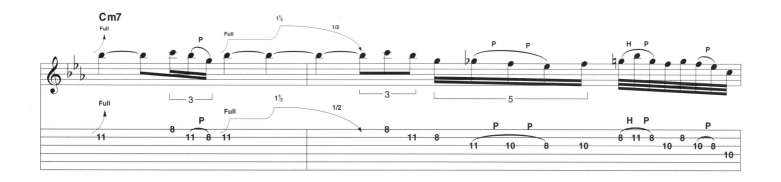

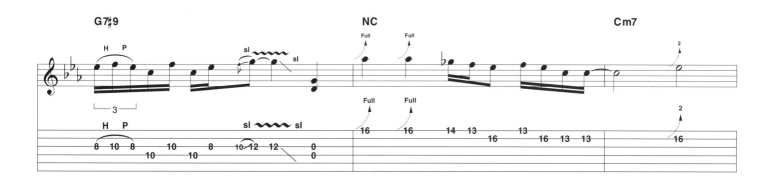

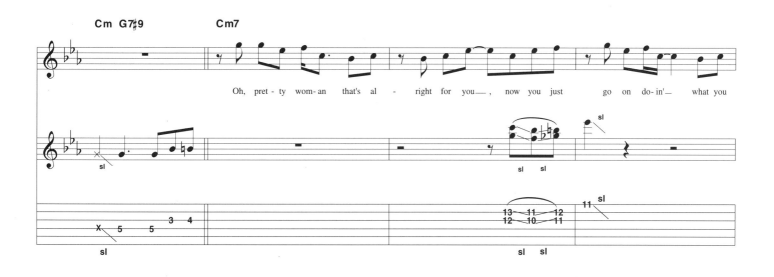

Oh, pret - ty wom- an that's al - right for you—, now you just go on do- in'— what you

wan- na do—. But some- day, when you think that you've got it made—, don't get in wide or deep e- nough so

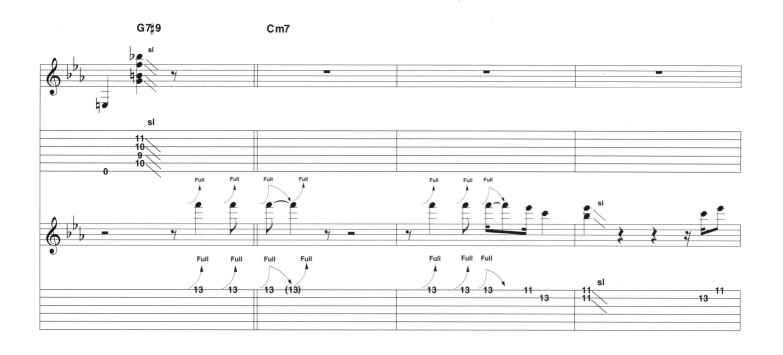

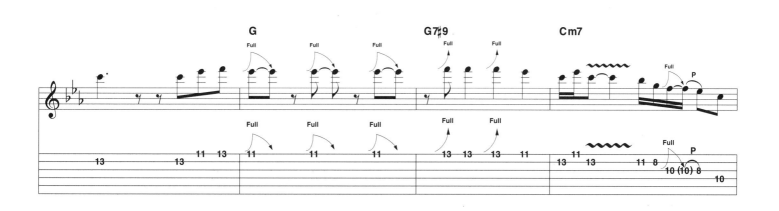

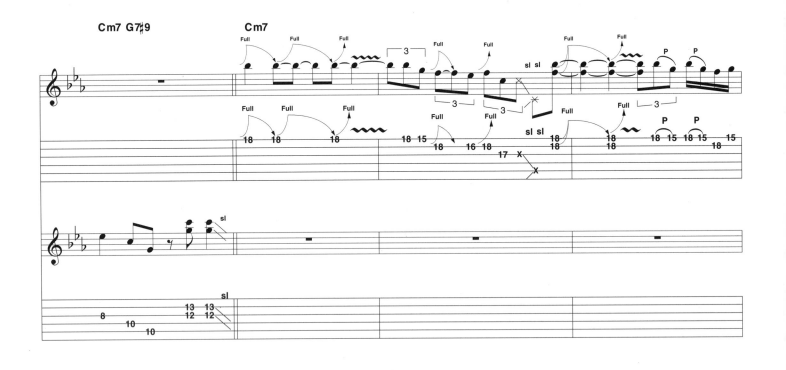

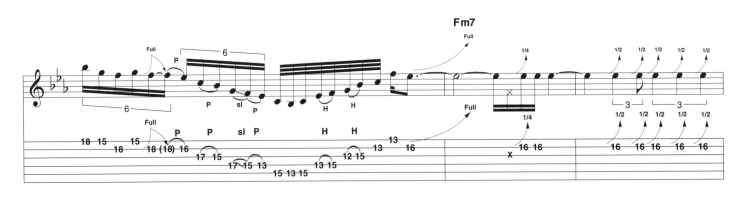

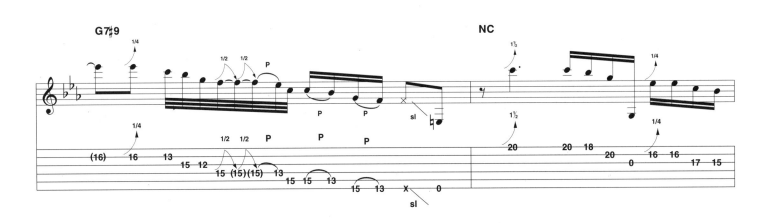

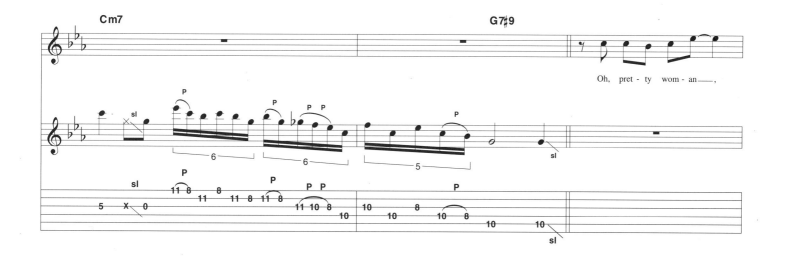

Oh, pret-ty wom-an——,

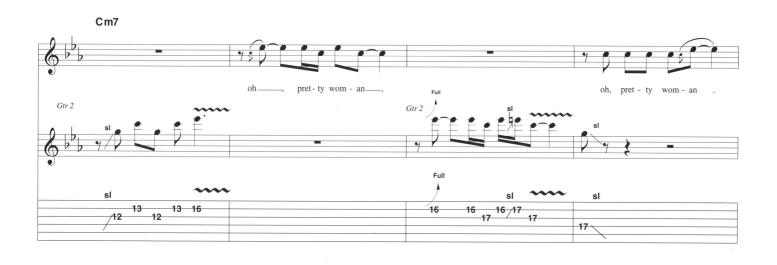

oh——, pret-ty wom-an——, oh, pret-ty wom-an .

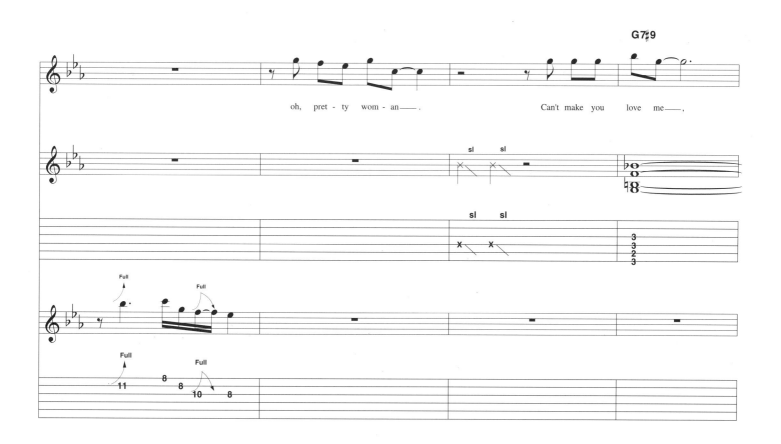

oh, pret-ty wom-an——. Can't make you love me——,

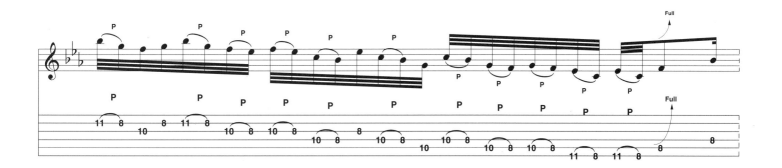

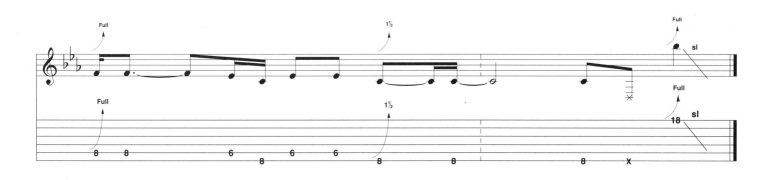

Story Of The Blues

Words and Music by GARY MOORE

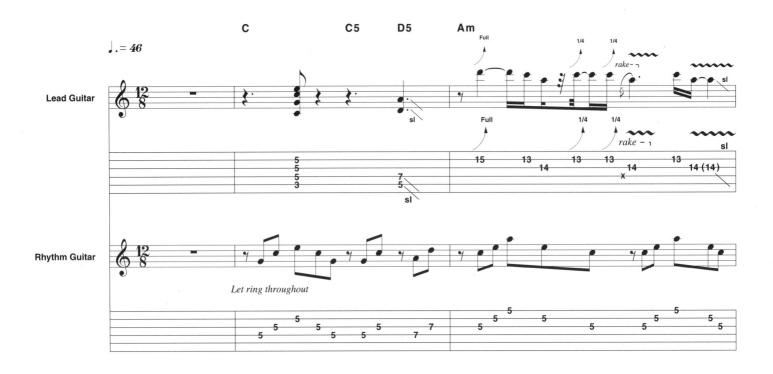

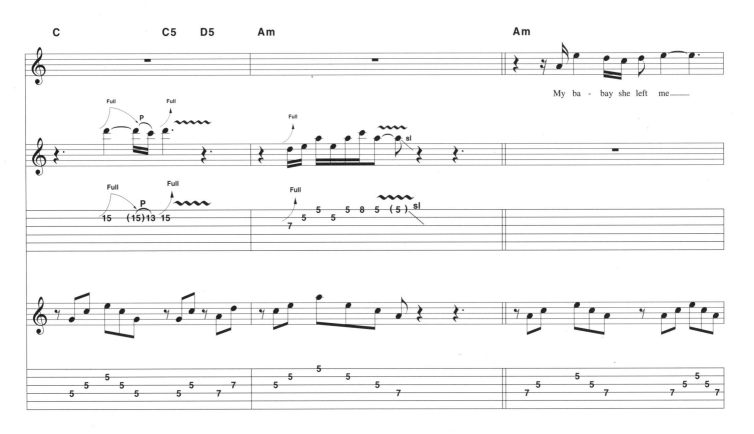

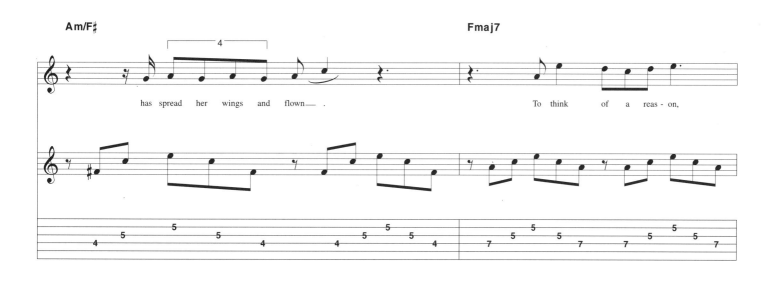

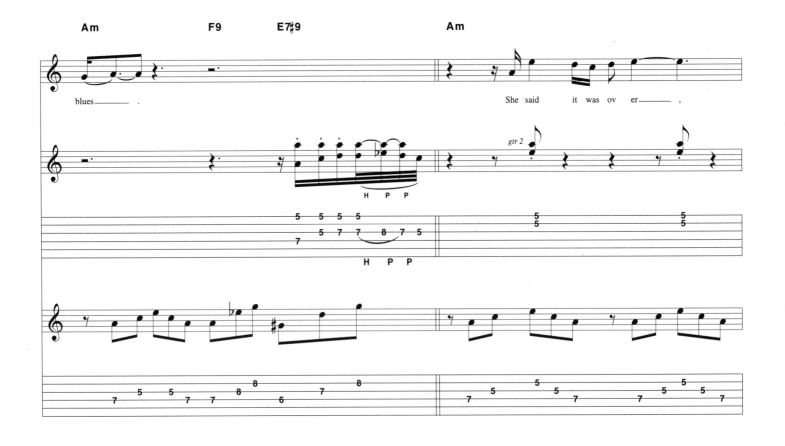

blues⸻ . She said   it was ov er⸻ ,

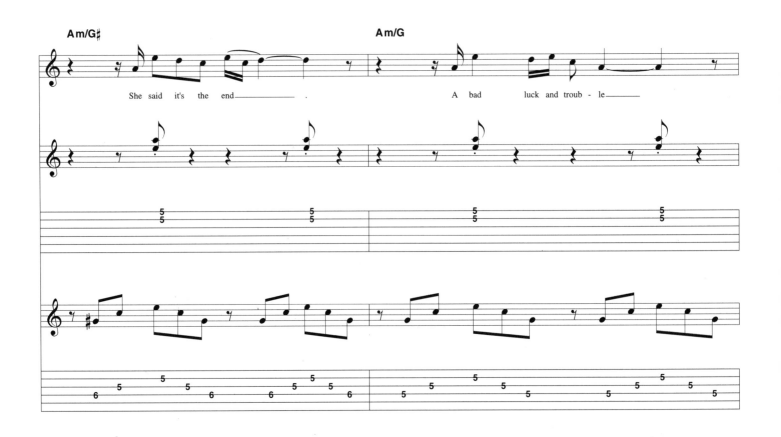

She said   it's   the   end⸻ . A   bad luck and troub - le⸻

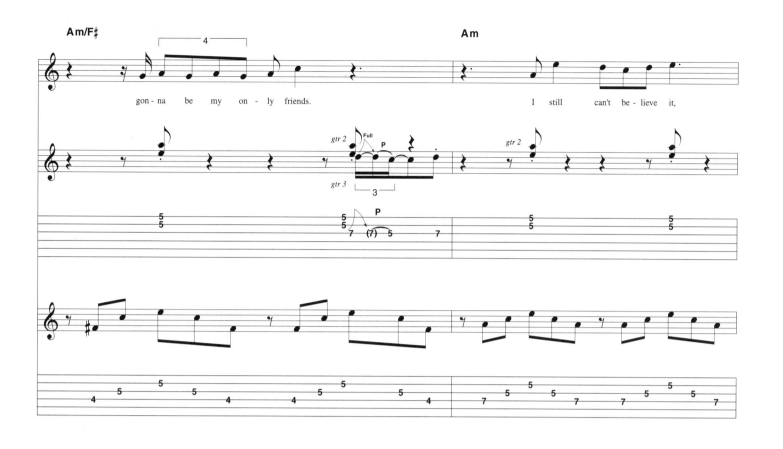

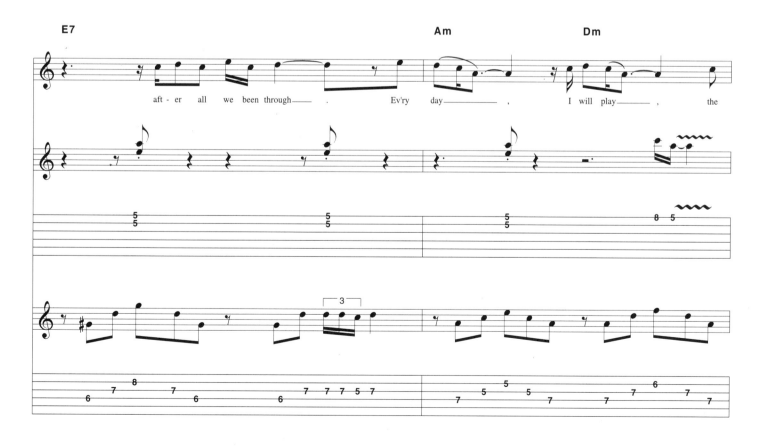

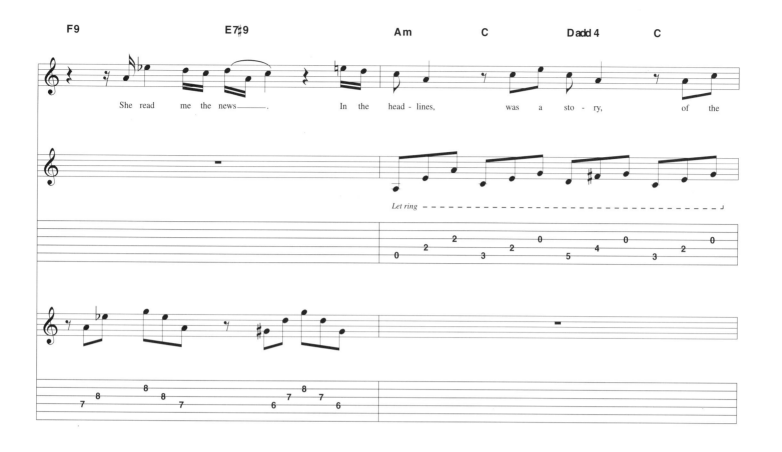

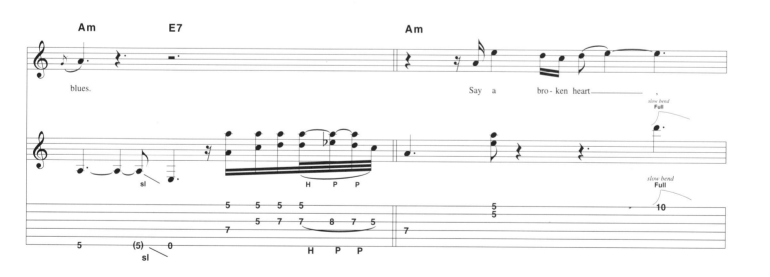

Am/G

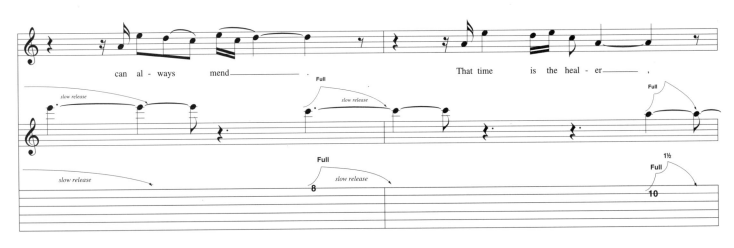

can al - ways mend————————, That time is the heal - er————,

and sad - ness will end———. But I've done so much cryin',

when will I laugh a - gain———? 'Till that day———, I will play——— the

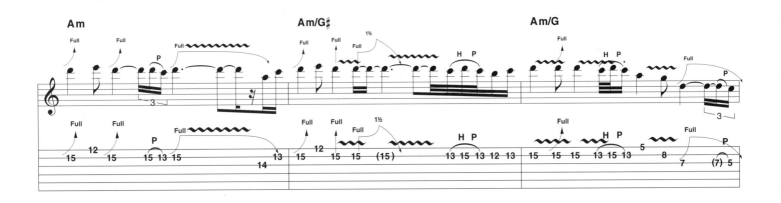

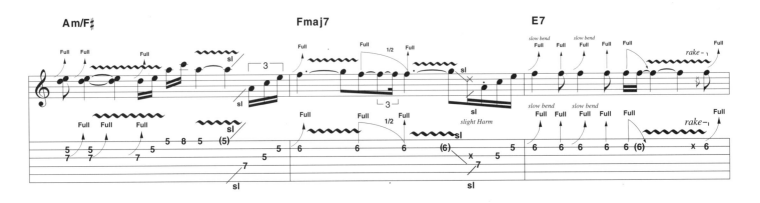

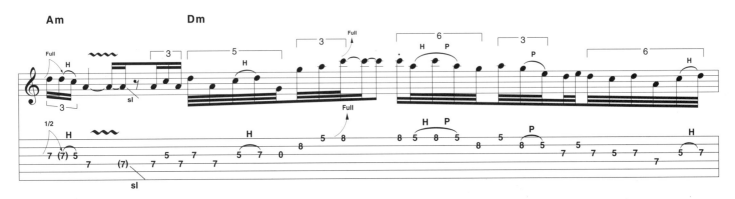

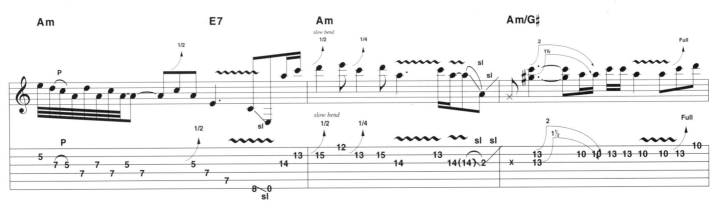

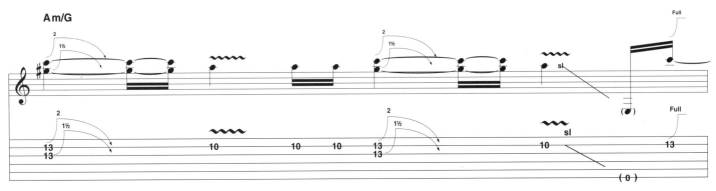

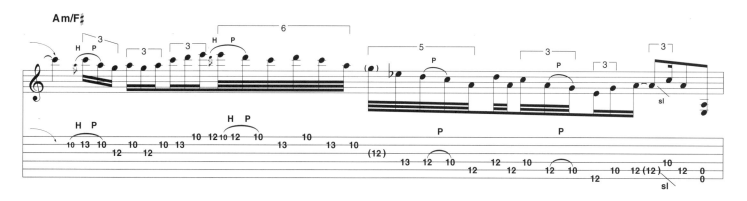

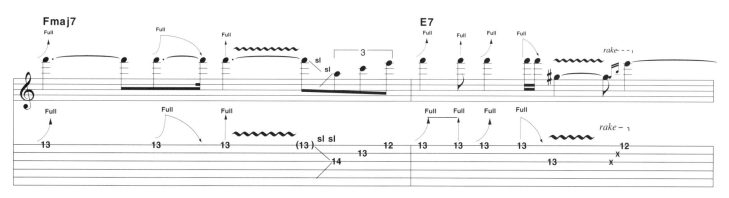

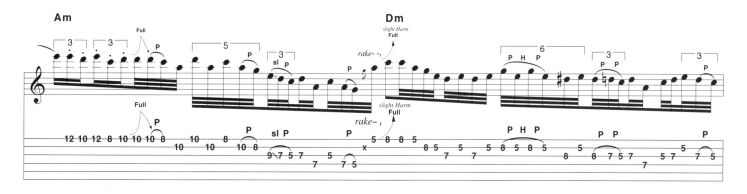

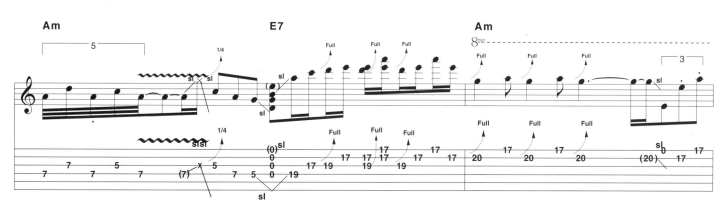

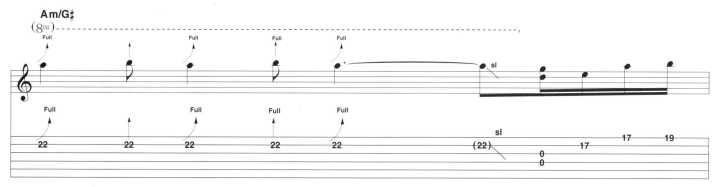

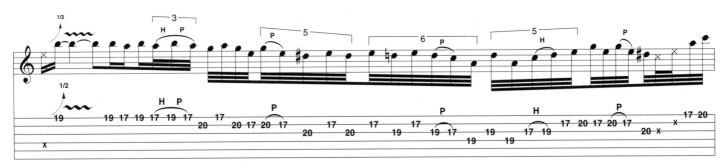

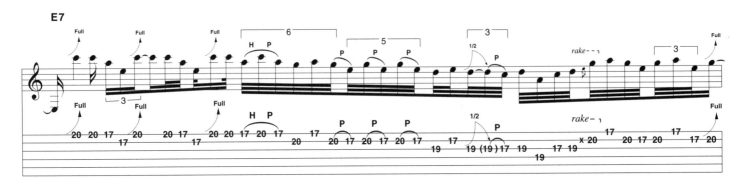

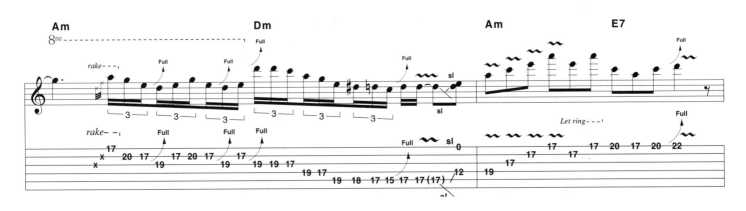

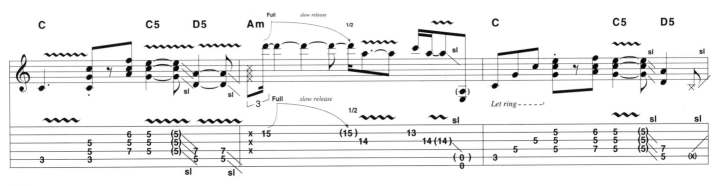

Cold Day In Hell

Words and Music by GARY MOORE

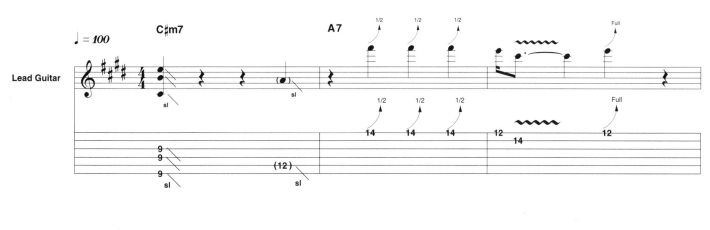

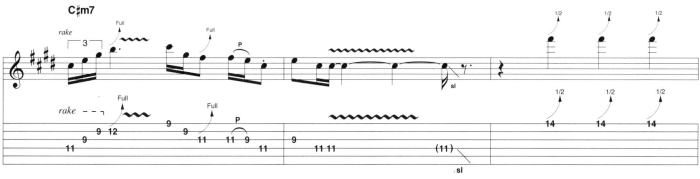

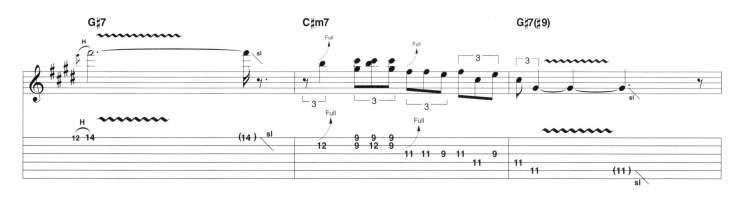

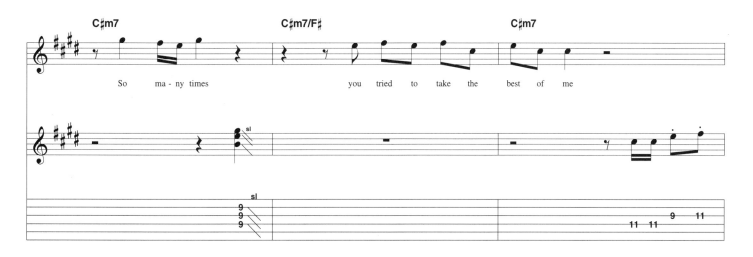

So ma-ny times   you tried to take the best of me

So many times   now you're gon-na   take   the rest

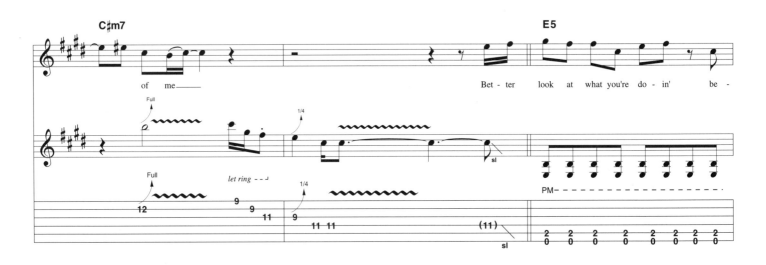

of me___   Bet-ter   look   at what you're do-in'   be-

fore it's too late___   It's a   fine   line you're tread-in'   be-tween   love and hate   There'll be a

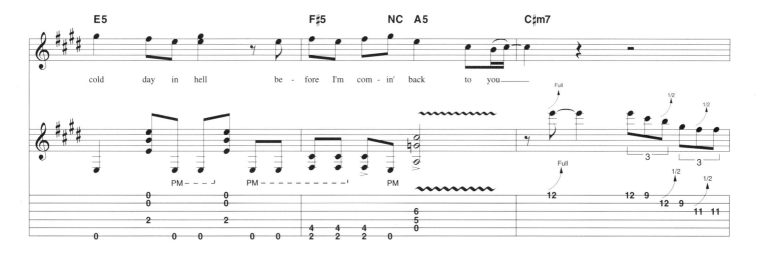

cold   day   in   hell   be - fore   I'm   com - in'   back   to   you____

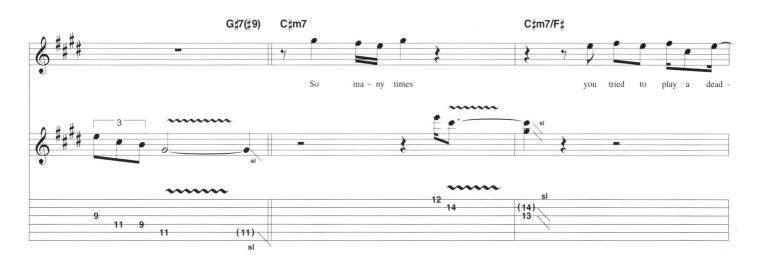

So   ma - ny   times   you   tried   to   play   a   dead -

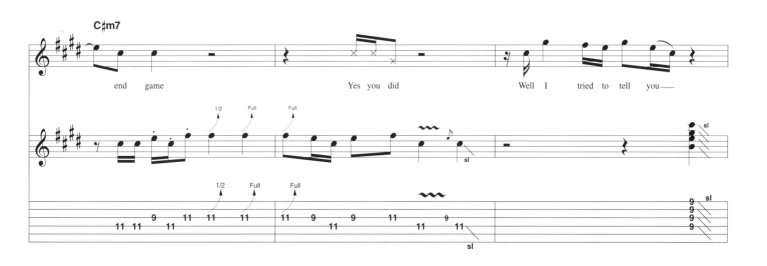

end   game   Yes   you   did   Well   I   tried   to   tell   you____

but you'd nev - er wan - na take the blame   Now you've

pushed me to the lim- it   and I can't take no more——   You bet ter take   one last look   be

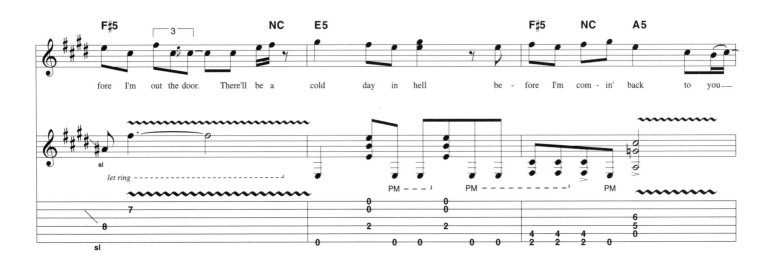

fore I'm out the door. There'll be a   cold   day   in hell   be - fore I'm com - in' back   to you——

60

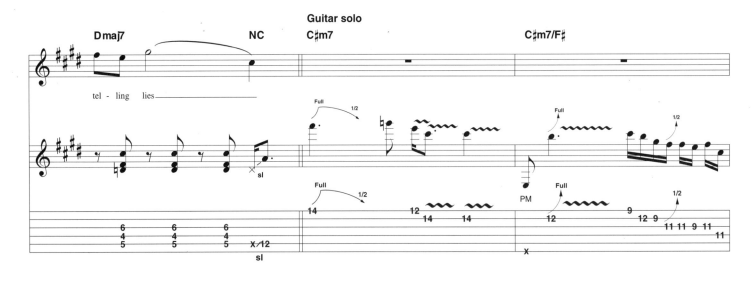

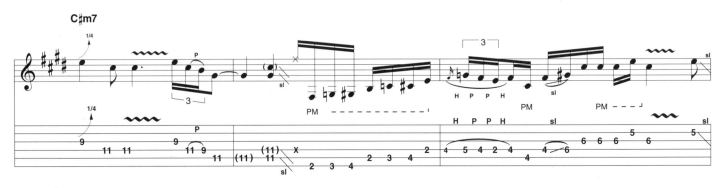

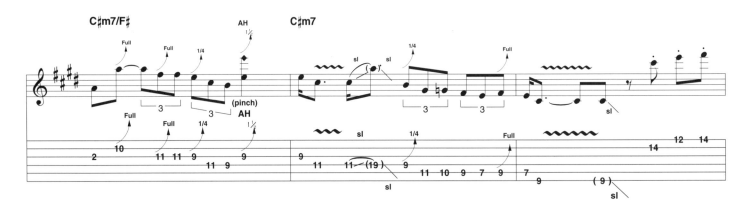

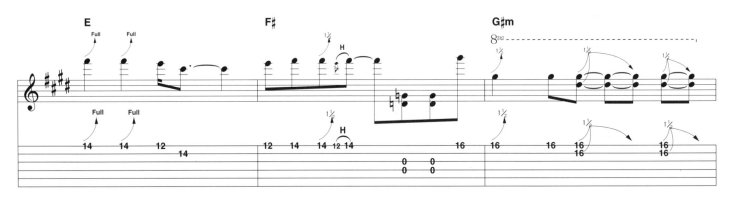

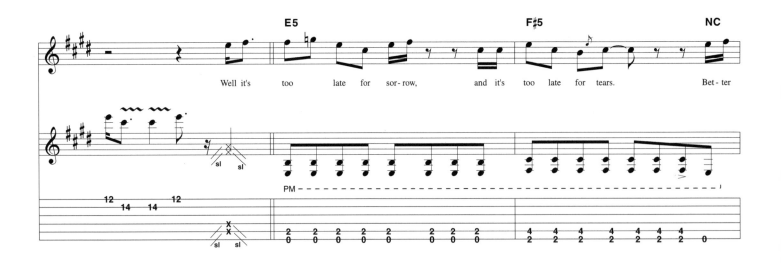

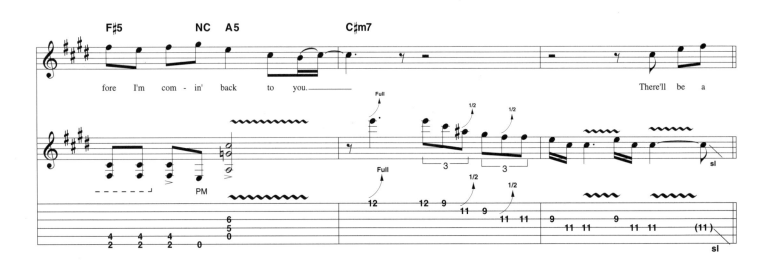

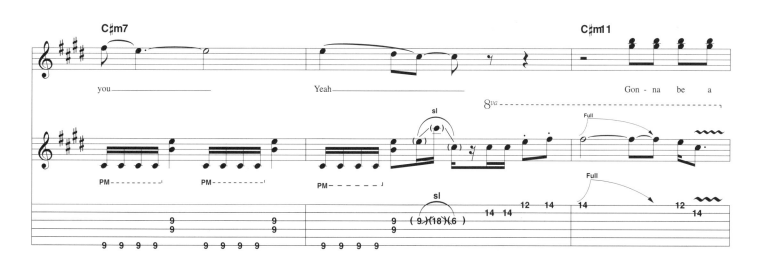

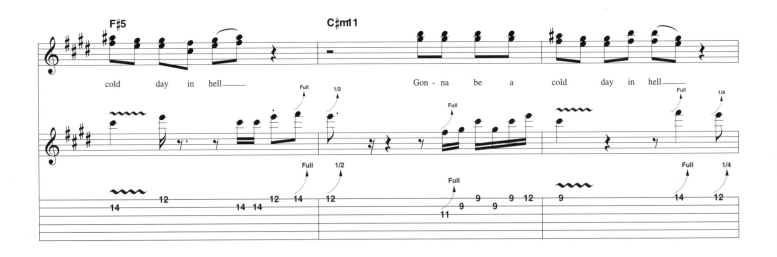

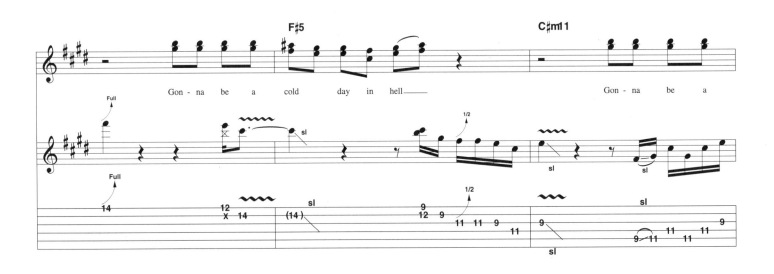

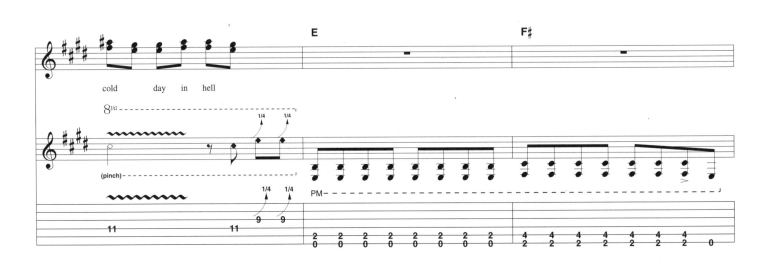

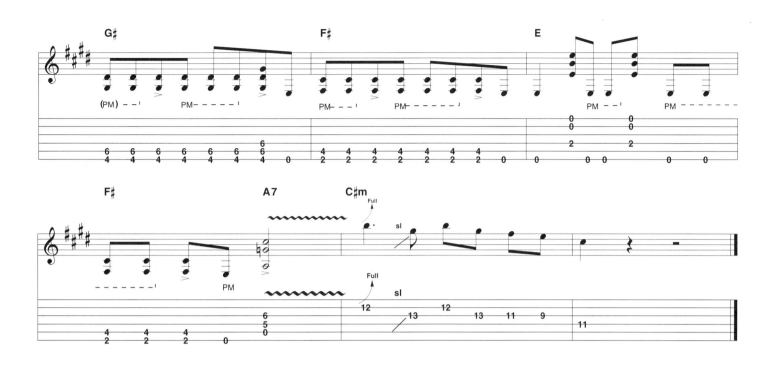

Empty Rooms

Words and Music by GARY MOORE and NEIL CARTER

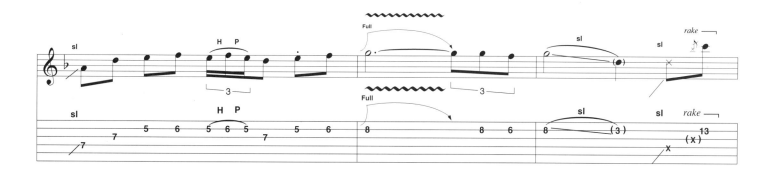
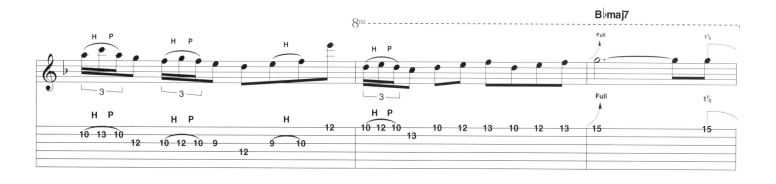
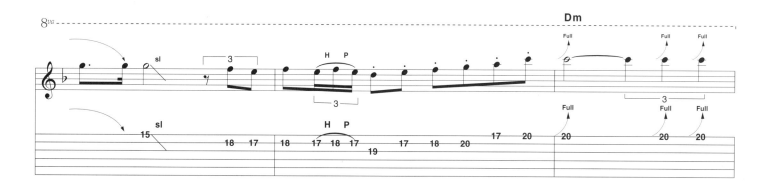
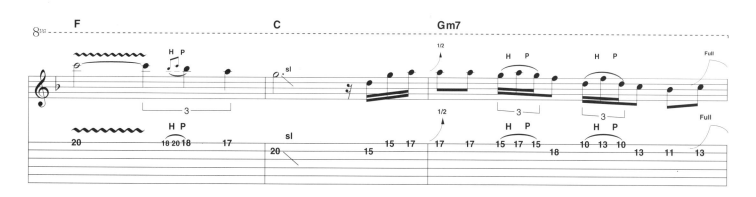
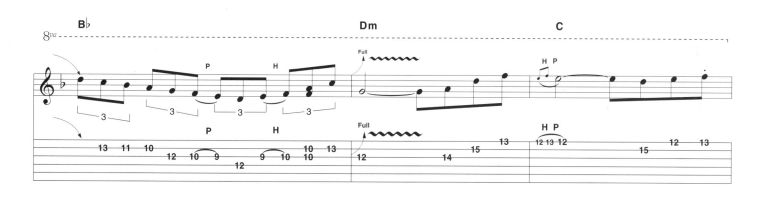

Parisienne Walkways

Words and Music by GARY MOORE and PHIL LYNOTT

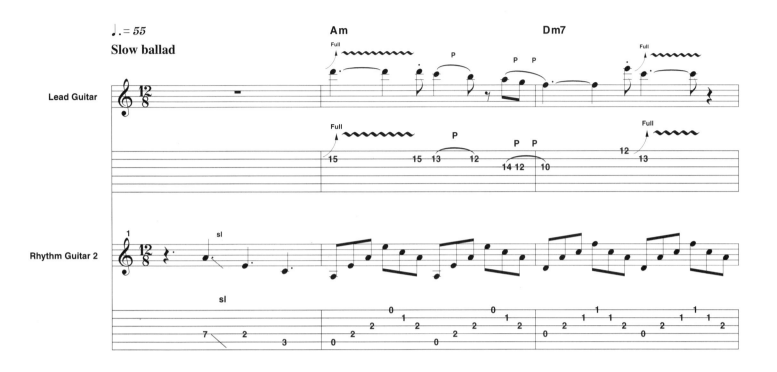

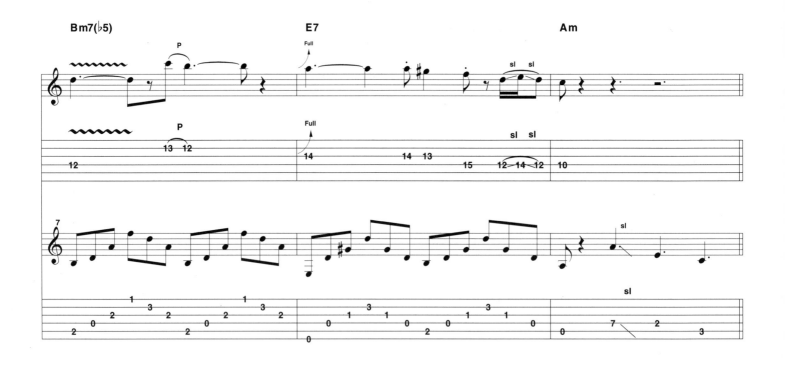

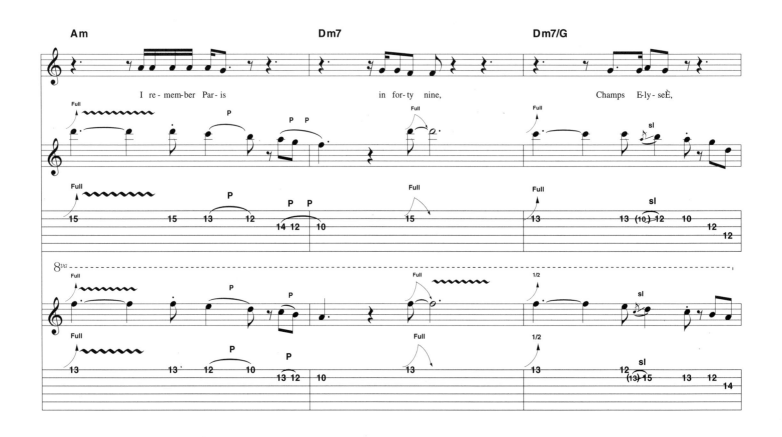

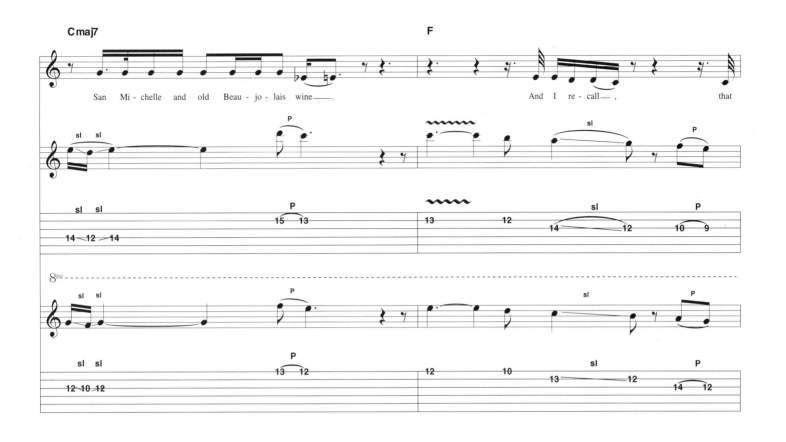

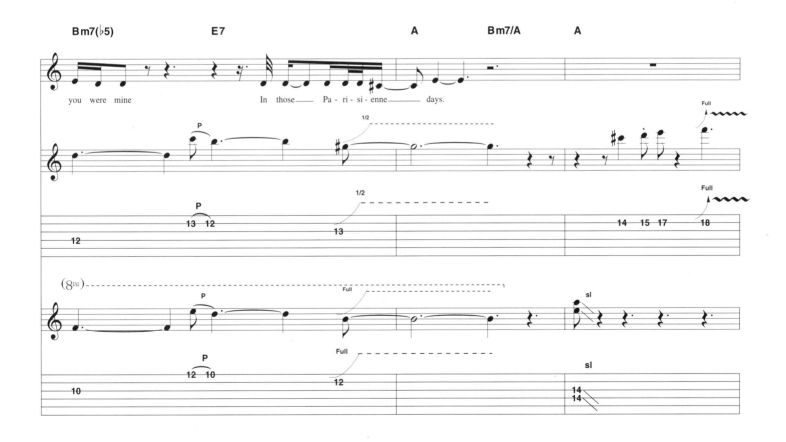

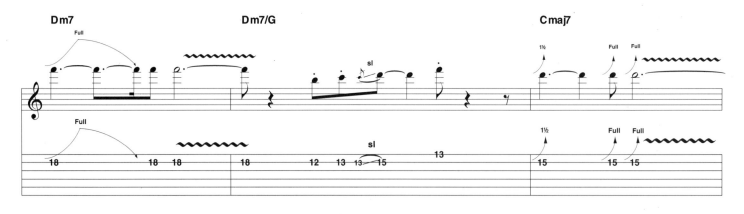

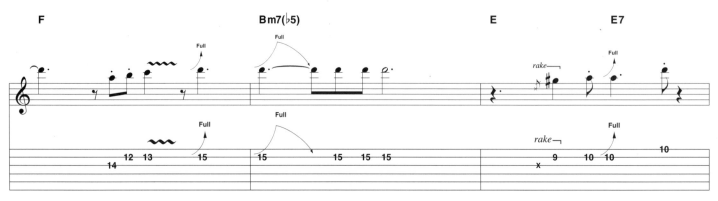

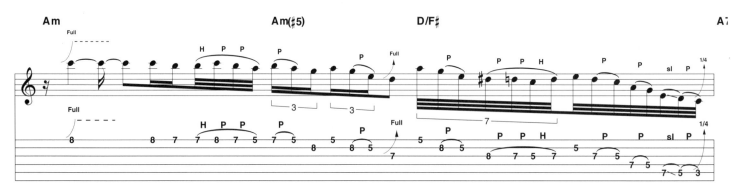

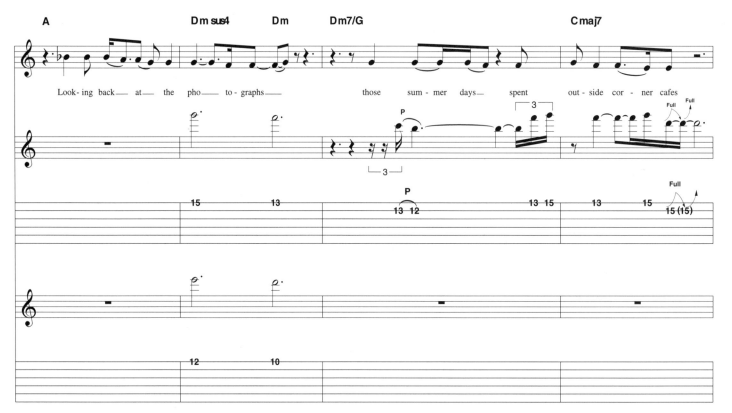

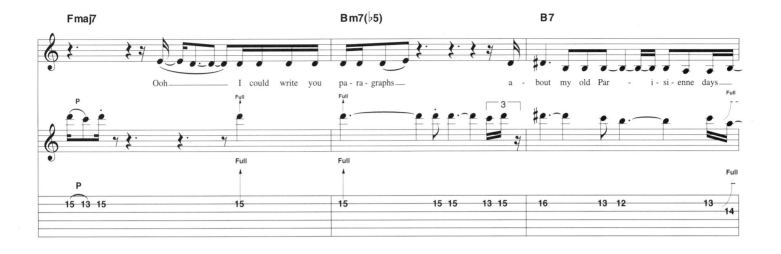

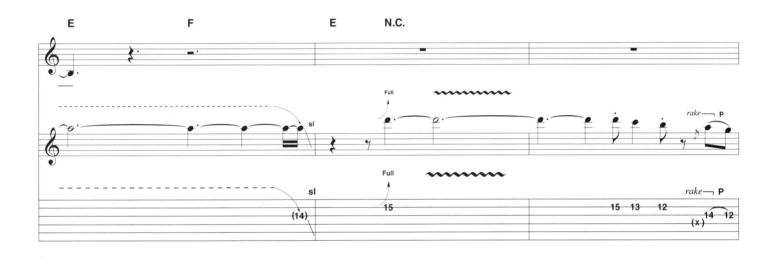

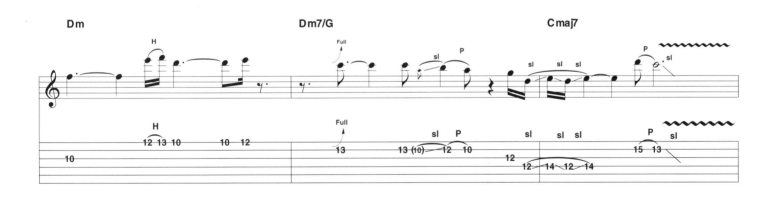

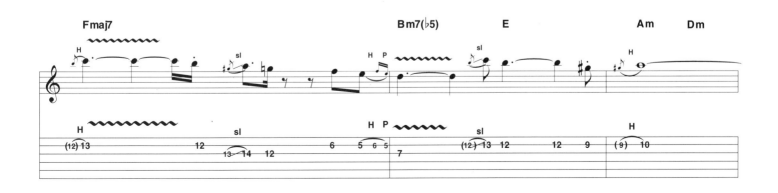

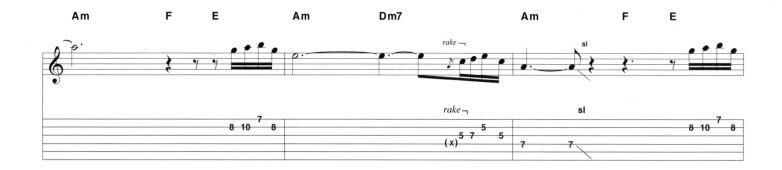

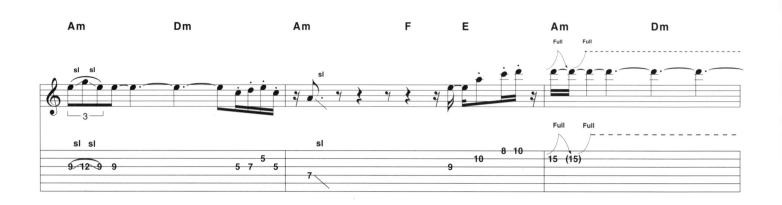

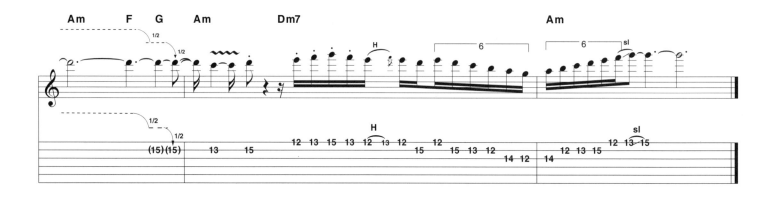

Printed and bound in Great Britain by Caligraving Ltd

THE JAM With SERIES
FROM FABER MUSIC

Each title includes complete transcriptions for guitar in musical notation and tablature *plus* superb quality backing tracks on CD prepared in **TOTAL ACCURACY** tradition minus lead guitar and vocals. In addition, for your reference, each CD contains *eight* extra tracks with all guitar parts added, so you can hear the rhythm, fills and solos as they should be played.

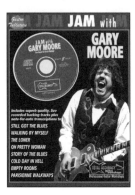

To buy Faber Music publications or to find out about the full range of titles available please contact your local music retailer or Faber Music sales enquiries:

Faber Music Ltd, Burnt Mill, Elizabeth Way, Harlow CM20 2HX
Tel: +44 (0) 1279 82 89 82   Fax: +44 (0) 1279 82 89 83
sales@fabermusic.com   fabermusic.com   expressprintmusic.com